MY DECADE
IN THE PREMIER LEAGUE

WAYNE ROONEY
MY DECADE
IN THE PREMIER LEAGUE

with Matt Allen

HarperSport
An Imprint of HarperCollins*Publishers*

HarperSport
An imprint of HarperCollins*Publishers*
77–85 Fulham Palace Road,
Hammersmith, London W6 8JB

www.harpercollins.co.uk

First published by HarperCollins*Publishers* 2012

2

A catalogue record of this book is
available from the British Library

HB ISBN 978-0-00-724263-4
PB ISBN 978-0-00-747652-7

Printed and bound in Great Britain by
Clays Ltd, St Ives plc

MIX
Paper from
responsible sources
FSC™ C007454

FSC™ is a non-profit international organisation established to promote
the responsible management of the world's forests. Products carrying the
FSC label are independently certified to assure consumers that they come
from forests that are managed to meet the social, economic and
ecological needs of present and future generations,
and other controlled sources.

Find out more about HarperCollins and the environment at
www.harpercollins.co.uk/green

CONTENTS

There are so many people who have helped and worked alongside me to make my Premier League dream become a reality. First and foremost my parents and family have played a massive role in getting me where I am today.

All the coaches and managers I have worked with since being a young lad, my agent Paul Stretford and the people who work alongside him, and all my team mates and friends in and out of the game: thanks for being there. But through working on this book and reflecting on the highs and lows of the last 10 years there are two people who merit specific mention.

To my wife Coleen, thanks for being there through the rough and the smooth; you will never know how much your love and support means to me. To my son Kai, you're my first thought in the morning and you give me my last smile at the end of the day. I love you both so much, you're my inspiration and my motivation every single day.

Thanks for everything.
Love,
Wayne (and Daddy) xxx

FOREWORD

BY SIR ALEX FERGUSON

There were plenty of eyebrows raised when I persuaded Manchester United's board of directors to sanction a multi-million pound move to try to prise away Wayne Rooney from Everton.

The lad was still only eighteen, but he had already shown in the two years he'd been in Everton's first team that he was a rare talent.

The Everton backroom staff had done a marvellous job nurturing the youngster through their academy to the day he made his debut for the first team when still some weeks short of his seventeenth birthday.

Long before he made his bow for the senior side everybody in the game was well aware that Everton had unearthed a little gem, and it didn't take him long to announce his arrival on the big stage.

Everton were Wayne's club as a schoolboy, so we can only imagine how he felt to pull on that famous royal blue shirt and run out to the roar of the Goodison Park crowd.

It wasn't a surprise that he took to first team football with the minimum of fuss. Wayne Rooney was born to play football and it was plain to see from the outset that his future as a major figure in the game was assured.

We were under no illusions that it would take anything other than a very, very large cheque if we were to tempt Everton into agreeing to let Wayne make the short move up the M62.

I suppose everyone has their price and eventually we managed to negotiate a deal with Everton to secure the services of the finest young player of his generation.

There's no question that it was a gigantic amount of money we paid for a player who hadn't long been eligible to vote, but we knew what we were doing.

Every so often a player comes along who is a racing certainty to make the grade as a professional, and Wayne Rooney was one of those.

It wasn't a gamble, it was an investment in the future, and there can be no doubt that the lad from Croxteth proceeded to pay off that outlay numerous times in the years that followed.

If anyone had any lingering doubts regarding our decision then they were almost instantly and conclusively dispelled when he scored a hat-trick on his debut in a Champions League group match against Turkish club Fenerbahçe at Old Trafford. Talk about starting the repayments early!

It wouldn't have bothered me if he'd taken weeks to score his first goal for us, but I've got to say I was overjoyed that he hit the ground running in classic style.

The rivalry between Manchester and Liverpool has been well documented over the years, but here was one Scouser who had immediately become an adopted Mancunian.

That was just the first few lines in a marvellous story that has continued to unfold during his career with Manchester United. He has become one of the mainstays of the club and is generally recognised as one of the finest players of the Premier League and Champions League era.

Wayne has also along the way ironed out the self-discipline problems he had as a youngster. Once looked upon as petulant and always likely to get in hot water with the authorities, he is now a reformed individual who sets the standards for the rest of the team.

It takes strength of character to overcome those types of personal traits, but he dug deep and eradicated what was a counter-productive part of his make-up.

Then there was his little wobble in the autumn of 2010, when he announced that he wanted to up sticks and leave Old Trafford.

I was shocked, and not a little disappointed, but it didn't take long to set him straight on that little matter and soon enough he was putting pen to paper on an extended contract.

I'm not about to say what was said between us during our discussions at that time, but I knew from the start that his heart was still with Manchester United and that all wasn't lost as we set about showing him the error of his thinking. Wayne Rooney has it within his grasp to carve for himself a very special place in the history of Manchester United.

He has already started overtaking long-standing club records, and with age on his side there are no limits to what he can achieve before the time comes for him to call it a day.

I'd like to think I've made one or two good decisions during my time in football – and a few I'd rather forget! – but there is no question that the signing of Wayne Rooney from Everton is right up there with the best of them.

INTRODUCTION

77 MINUTES, 19 SECONDS

Bang!

Everything goes dead mad, dead quick.

Then that feeling kicks in – an unbelievable feeling of satisfaction that I get from scoring a goal in the Premier League. Like the sensation I get whenever I've smashed a golf ball flush off the face of the club and watched it trickle onto the green.

It's a high – a mad rush of power.

It's a wave of emotion – but it takes me over like nothing else.

This feeling of putting one away for Manchester United is huge, selfish, nuts. I reckon if I could bottle the buzz, I'd be able to make the best energy drink ever.

A heartbeat later and I'm at normal speed again, I'm coming round.

Everything's in focus: the sound, a roar loud enough to hurt my ears, like a plane taking off; the aching in my legs, the sweat running down my neck, the mud on my kit. There's more and more noise; it's so big, it's right on top of me. Someone's grabbing at my shirt, my heart's banging out of my chest. The crowd are singing my name:

'Rooney!'
'Rooney!'
'Rooooo-neeee!'

And there's no better feeling in the world.

Then I look up and see the scoreboard.

12 FEBRUARY 2011
United **2**   City **1**
GOAL!
Rooney, 77 minutes

Who I am and what I've done comes back to me in a rush, a hit, like a boxer coming round after a sniff of smelling salts. I'm Wayne Rooney. I've played Premier League football since 2002 and I've just scored the winning goal in a Manchester derby – probably the most important game of the season to fans from the red half of town. A goal that puts our noisy neighbours, the other lot, in their place. A goal that reminds them that United have more history and more success than they do right now. A goal that warns the rest of the country that we're on our way to winning another Premier League title.

The best goal of my career.

As I stand with my arms spread wide, head back, I can feel the hate coming from the City fans in the stand behind me, it's like static electricity. The abuse, the screaming and swearing, is bouncing off me. They're sticking their fingers up at me, red-faced. They've all got a cob on, but I don't give a toss. I know how much they hate me, how angry they are; I can understand where they're coming from though, because I go through the same emotions whenever I lose at anything.

This time, they're wound up and I'm not.

I know it doesn't get any better than this.

I've bagged hundreds of goals during my time in the Premier League with United and Everton; goals in league games, cup games, cup finals, meaningless friendlies, practice games in training. But this one is extra special. As I jog back to the centre circle, still tingling, I go into rewind. It's ridiculous, I know, but I'm worried I might never feel this way again. I want to remember what's just happened, to relive the moment over and over because it feels so good.

We were under pressure, I know that, the game level at 1–1, really tight. In the seconds before the goal, I try to lay a return pass back to my strike partner, Dimitar Berbatov – a ringer for Andy Garcia in *The Godfather Part III*; dangerous like Andy Garcia in *The Godfather Part III* – but my touch is heavy. I overhit it. My heart jumps into my mouth.

City can break from here.

Luckily, Paul Scholes – ginger lad, low centre of gravity, the fella we call SatNav because his passes seem almost computer controlled, probably the best midfielder ever to play in the Premier League – scoops up the loose ball and plays it out to our winger, Nani, on the edge of the box. He takes a couple of touches, guiding the ball with his toes, gliding over the grass more like a dancer off *Strictly Come Dancing* than a footy player, and curls a pass over the top of the City defence towards me, his cross deflecting off a defender, taking some speed off it.

I see a space opening up in the penalty area. City's two man-mountain centre-halves, Joleon Lescott and Vincent Kompany, move and get ready for the incoming pass. I run into a few yards of space, guessing where the ball will land. My senses are all over the place.

It's hard to explain to someone who's never played the game or felt the pressure of performing in front of a big crowd before, but playing football at Old Trafford is like running around in a bubble. It's really intense, claustrophobic.

I can smell the grass, I can hear the crowd, but I can't make out what's being sung. Everything's muffled, like when I'm underwater in the swimming baths: I can hear the shouting and splashing from everyone around me in the pool, but nothing's clear, I can't pick out any one voice. I can't really hear what people are yelling.

It's the same on the pitch. I can hear certain sounds when the game slows down for a moment or two, like when I'm taking a corner or free-kick and there's a strange rumble of 20,000 spring-loaded seats thwacking back in a section of the ground behind me as I stand over the ball, everyone on their feet, craning their necks to watch. But it's never long before the muffled noise comes over again. Then I'm back underwater. Back in the bubble.

The ball's coming my way.

The deflection has changed the shape of Nani's pass, sending it higher than I thought, which buys me an extra second to shift into position and re-adjust my balance, to think: *I'm having a go at this.* My legs are knackered, but I use all the strength I have to spring from the back of my heels, swinging my right leg over my left shoulder in mid-air to bang the cross with an overhead kick, an acrobatic volley. It's an all or nothing hit that I know will make me look really stupid if I spoon it.

But I don't.

I make good contact with the ball and it fires into the top corner; I feel it, but I don't see it. As I twist in mid-air, trying to follow the flight of my shot, I can't see where the ball has gone, but the sudden roar of noise tells me I've scored. I roll over and see Joe Hart, City's goalkeeper, rooted to the spot, his arms spread wide in disbelief, the ball bobbling and spinning in the net behind him.

If playing football is like being underwater, then scoring a goal feels like coming up for air.

I can see and hear it all, clear as anything. Faces in the crowd, thousands and thousands of them shouting and smiling, climbing over one another. Grown men jumping up and down like little kids. Children screaming with proper passion, flags waving. Every image is razor sharp. I see the colour of the stewards' bibs in the stands. I can see banners hanging from the Stretford End: 'For Every Manc A Religion'; 'One Love'. It's like going from black and white to colour; standard to high-definition telly at a push of the remote.

Everyone is going mental in the crowd; they think the game is just about won.

From nearly giving the ball away to smashing a winning goal into the top corner: it's scary how fine the margins are in top-flight footy. The difference between winning and losing is on a knife edge a lot of the time. That's why it's the best game in the world.

*****

We close out the game 2–1. Everyone gathers round me in the dressing room afterwards, they want to talk about the goal. But I'm wrecked, done in, I've got nothing left; it's all out there on the pitch, along with that overhead kick. The room is buzzing; Rio Ferdinand is buzzing.

'Wow,' he says.

Patrice Evra, our full-back, calls it 'beautiful'.

Then The Manager comes into the dressing room, his big black coat on; he looks made up, excited. The man who has shouted, screamed and yelled from the Old Trafford touch-lines for over a quarter of a century; the man who has managed and inspired some of the greatest players in Premier League history. The man who signed me for the biggest club in the world. *The most successful club boss in the modern game.*

He walks round to all of us and shakes our hands like he does after every win. It's been like this since the day I signed for United. Thankfully I've had a lot of handshakes.

He lets on to me. 'That was magnificent, Wayne, that was great.'

I nod; I'm too tired to speak, but I wouldn't say anything if I could.

Don't get me wrong, there's nothing better than The Manager saying well done – but I don't need it. I know when I've played well and when I've played badly. I don't think, *If The Manager says I've played well, I've played well*. I know in my heart whether I have or I haven't.

Then he makes out that it's the best goal he's ever seen at Old Trafford. He should know, he's been around the club long enough and seen plenty of great goalscorers come and go during his time.

The Manager is in charge of everything and he controls the players at Manchester United emotionally and physically. Before the game he reads out the teamsheet and I sometimes get that same weird, nervous feeling I used to get whenever the coach of the school team pinned the starting XI to the noticeboard. During a match, if we're a goal down but playing well, he tells us to keep going. He knows an equaliser is coming. He talks us into winning. Then again, I've known us to be winning by two or three goals at half-time and he's gone nuts when we've sat down in the dressing room.

We're winning. What's up with him?

Then I cotton on.

He doesn't want us to be complacent.

Like most managers he appreciates good football, but he appreciates winners more. His desire to win is greater than in anyone I've ever known, and it rubs off on all of us.

The funny thing is, I think we're quite similar. We both have a massive determination to succeed and that has a lot to do with our upbringing – as kids we were told that if we wanted to do well we'd have to fight for it and graft. That's the way I was brought up; I think it was the way he was brought up, too. And when we win something, like a Premier League title or the Champions League trophy, we're stubborn enough to hang onto that success. That's why we work so hard, so we can be the best for as long as possible.

Everyone begins to push and shove around a small telly in the corner of the room. It's been sitting there for years and the coaches always turn it on to replay the game whenever there's been a controversial incident or maybe a penalty shout that hasn't been given – and there's been a few of those, as The Manager will probably tell anyone who wants to listen. This time, I want to see my goal. Everyone does.

One of the coaches grabs the controls and forwards the action to the 77th minute.

I see my heavy touch, Scholesy's pass to Nani.

I see his cross.

Then I watch, like it's a weird out of body experience, as I throw myself up in the air and thump the ball into the back of the net. It doesn't seem real.

I reckon all footballers go to bed and dream about scoring great goals: dribbling the ball around six players and popping it over the goalkeeper, or smashing one in from 25 yards. Scoring from a bicycle kick is one I've always fantasised about.

I've just scored a dream goal in a Manchester derby.

'Wow,' says Rio, for the second time, shaking his head.

I know what he means. I sit in the dressing room, still sweating, trying to live in the moment for as long as I can because these moments are so rare. I can still hear the United fans singing outside, giving it to the City lot, and I wonder if I'll ever score a goal as good as that again.

*****

I've played in the Premier League for 10 years now. I'm probably in the middle of my career, which feels weird. The time has flown by so quickly. It does my head in a little, but I still reckon my best years are ahead of me, that there's plenty more to come. It only seems like five minutes ago that I was making my debut for Everton against Tottenham in August 2002. The Spurs fans were tucked away in one end of Goodison Park. When I ran onto the pitch they started singing at me:

'Who are ya?'

Whenever I touched the ball:

'Who are ya?'

They don't sing that at me anymore. They just boo and chuck abuse and slag me off instead. Funny that.

In the 10 years since my debut, I've done a hell of a lot. From 2002 to 2004 I played for Everton, the team I supported as a boy; I became the youngest player to represent England in 2003, before Arsenal's Theo Walcott had that record off me. In 2004 I signed for Man United for a fee in excess of £25 million and became the club's highest-ever Premier League goalscorer. During the European Championships that same year, the England players nicknamed me 'Wazza'; the title seems to have stuck.

I've won four Premier League titles, a Champions League, two League Cups, three FA Community Shields and a FIFA Club World Cup. I've scored over 200 goals for club and country, and been sent off five times. I'd be lying if I told you that I haven't loved every minute of it. Well, OK, maybe not the red cards and the suspensions, but everything else has been sound.

The funny thing is, the excitement and adrenaline I felt on the night before my league debut for Everton in 2002 still gets to me. The day before a game, home or away, always feels like Christmas Eve. When I go to bed I'll wake up two or three times in the night and roll over to look at the alarm clock.

Gutted. It's only two in the morning.

The buzz and the anticipation are there until the minute we kick off.

I've paid the price, though. Physically I've taken a bit of a battering over the years; being lumped by Transformersized centre-backs or having my muscles smashed by falls, shoulder barges and last-ditch tackles, day in, day out, has left me a bit bruised.

When I get up in the morning after a game, I struggle to walk for the first half an hour. I ache a bit. It wasn't like that when I was a lad. I remember sometimes when I finished training or playing with Everton and United, I'd want to play some more. There was a small-sided pitch in my garden and I used to play in there with my mates. When I trained with Everton, I used to go for a game down the local leisure centre afterwards, or we used to play in the street in Croxteth, the area of Liverpool where I grew up with my mum, dad and younger brothers Graham and John. There was a nursery facing my house. When it closed for the day, they'd bring some shutters down which made for a handy goal. I loved playing there. After I'd made my England debut in 2003 I was photographed kicking a ball against that nursery in a France shirt.

Footy has had a massive impact on my body because my game is based on speed and power. Intensity. As a striker I need to work hard all the time; I need to be sharp, which means my fitness has to be right to play well. If it isn't, it shows. It would probably be different if I were a full-back; I could hide a bit, make fewer runs into the opposition's half and get away with it. As a centre-forward for Manchester United, there's no place to hide. I've got to work as hard as I can, otherwise The Manager will haul me off the pitch or drop me for the next game. There's no room for failure or second best at this club.

If there is a downside to my life then it's the pressure of living in the public eye. I'd like just for one day to have no-one know me at all, to do normal stuff; to be able to go to the shops and not have everyone stare and take pictures. Even just to be able to go for a night out with my mates and not have anyone point at me would be nice. On a weekend, some of my pals go to the betting shop before the matches start and put down a little bet – I'd love to be able to do that. But look, this is the small stuff, I'm grateful for everything that football has given me.

There is one small paranoia: like any player I'm fearful of getting a career-ending injury. I could be in the best form of my life and then one day a bad tackle might finish my time in the sport. It's over then. But I think that's the risk I take as a player in every match. I know football is such a short career that one day, at any age, the game could be snatched from me unexpectedly. But *I* want to decide when I leave football, not a physio, or an opponent's boot.

Don't get me wrong, the fear of injury or failure has never got into my head when I've been playing. I've never frozen on the football pitch. I've always wanted to express myself, I've always wanted to try things. I've never gone into a game worrying.

I hope we don't lose this one.

What's going to happen if we get beat?

I've always been confident that we're going to win the game, whoever I've played for. I've never been short of belief in a game of footy.

I'm so confident, I'm happy to play anywhere on the pitch. I've offered to play centre-back when United have been hit by injuries; I've even offered to play full-back. I reckon I could go there and do a good job, no problem. I remember Edwin van der Sar once busted his nose against Spurs and had to go off. We didn't have a reserve goalie and I thought about going in nets because I played there in training a few times and I'd done alright. Against Portsmouth in the FA Cup in 2008, our keeper Tomasz Kuszczak was sent off and I wanted to go in then, but The Manager made me stay up top because Pompey were about to take a pen. I could see his point. Had I been in goal I wouldn't have been able to work up front for the equaliser.

When I was a lad, I thought I'd be able to play football forever. These days, I know it's not going to last, but the funny thing is I'm not too worried about the end of my career, the day I have to jack it all in. If I'm ever at a stage where I feel I'm not performing as well as I used to, then I'll take an honest look at myself. I'll work out whether I'm still able to make a difference in matches at the highest level. I'm not going to hang around to snatch the odd game here and there in the Premier League. I'll play abroad somewhere, maybe America. I'd love to have a go at coaching if the opportunity comes up.

The thing is, I want to be remembered for playing well in football's best teams, like United. I want to burn out brightly on the pitch at Old Trafford, not fade away on the subs' bench.

*****

Hanging up my footy boots is a way off yet. There's more stuff to be won. I want more league titles, more Champions Leagues – anything United are playing for, I want to win it. I'm into winning titles for the team because winning personal achievements, while being nice, isn't the same as winning trophies with my teammates. And whatever I do, I do it to be the best that I can. I'm not good at being an also-ran, as anyone who has played with me will know.

For 10 years, it's been all or nothing for me in the Premier League.

CHAPTER

1

DESIRE

Ten years in the Premier League. All the goals and trophies, injuries and bookings driven by one thought: I hate losing. I hate it with a passion. It's the worst feeling ever and not even a goal or three in a match can make a defeat seem OK. Unless I've walked off the pitch a winner, the goals are pointless. If United lose, I'm not interested in how many I've scored.

I'm so bad that I even hate the thought of losing. Thinking about defeat annoys me, it does my head in, it's not an option for me, but when it does happen, *I* lose it. I get angry, I see red, I shout at teammates, I throw things and I sulk. I hate the fact that I act this way, but I can't help it. I was a bad loser as a lad playing games with my brothers and mates, and I'm a bad loser now, playing for United.

It doesn't matter where I'm playing, or who I'm playing against either, I'm the same every time I put on my footy boots. In a practice match at Carrington before the last game of the 2009/10 season, I remember being hacked down in the area twice. I remember it because it annoys me so much. The ref, one of our fitness coaches, doesn't give me a decision all game and my team loses by a couple of goals. When the final whistle blows and the rest of the lads walk back to the dressing room to get changed, laughing and joking together, I storm off in a mood, kicking training cones and slamming doors.

It's the same when I'm competing off the pitch. I often play computer games with the England lads when I'm away on international duty. One time I lose a game of FIFA and throw a control pad across the room afterwards because I'm so annoyed with myself. Another night I lean forward and turn the machine off in the middle of a game because I know I'm going to lose. Everyone stares at me like I'm a head case.

'Come on, Wazza, don't be like that.'

That annoys me even more, so I boot everyone out of the room and sulk on my own.

It's not just my teammates I lose it with. I have barneys with people as far away as Thailand and Japan when I play them at a football game online. They beat me; I argue with them on the headset that links the players through an internet connection. I'm a grown man. Maybe I should relax a bit more, but I find it hard to cool down when things aren't going my way, and besides, everyone's like that in my family. We're dead competitive. Board games, tennis in the street, whatever it was that we played when I was a lad, we played to win. And none of us liked losing.

I sometimes think it's a good thing – I don't reckon I'd be the same as a footballer if I was happy to settle for second best. I need this desire to push me on when I'm playing, like Eric Cantona and Roy Keane did when they were at United. They had proper passion. I do too, it gives me an edge, it pushes me on to try harder. Those two couldn't stand to lose. They didn't exactly make many pals on the pitch either, but they won a lot of trophies. I'm the same. I doubt many players would say they've enjoyed competing with me in the past and I like to think that I'm a pain in the backside for everyone I play against. I'm probably a pain in the backside for people I play with as well, because when United lose or look like losing a game at half-time, I go mad in the dressing room.

I scream and shout.

I boot a ball across the room.

I throw my boots down.

I lose it with teammates.

I yell at people and they yell at me.

I'm not shouting and screaming and kicking footballs across the room because I don't like someone. I'm doing it because I respect them and I want them to play better.

I can't stand us being beaten.

I yell at players, they yell at me. I don't take it personally when I'm getting a rollicking and I don't expect people to take it personally when I dish it out to them. It's all part of the game. Yeah, it feels like a curse sometimes, the anger and moodiness when I lose, but it's an energy. It makes me the player that I am.

*****

My hatred of losing, of being second best, starts in Croxteth. My family are proud; Crocky is a proud place and nobody wants to let themselves down or their family down in the street where I live. My family haven't got a lot, but we have enough to get through and my brothers and I aren't allowed to take anything for granted as we're growing up. We know that if we want something, we have to graft for it and I'm told that rewards shouldn't come easily. I pick that up from my mum, my dad, my nan and my granddad. I learn that if I work hard, I'll earn rewards. If I try at school, I'll get the latest Everton shirt – the team my whole family supports – or a new footy if I need one. It's where the will to work comes from.

This discipline, the desire to win and push myself, also happens away from school. I box at the Crocky Sports Centre with my Uncle Richie, a big bloke with a flat boxer's nose. He hits pretty hard. I never actually scrap properly but I spar three times a week and the training gives me strength and an even harder competitive streak. Most of all it brings out my self belief.

I think we're all confident in the family, but I don't think it's just the Rooneys. I reckon it's a Liverpool thing. Everyone's really outgoing in Crocky; everyone speaks their mind, which I like. As a kid, I learn to take that self-belief into the boxing gym. If ever I get into the ring with a lad twice my size I never think, *Look at the size of him! I'm going to get battered.* Doing that means I'm beat in my head already. Instead, I go into every fight thinking, *I'm going to win*, even against the bigger lads. One pal at the gym is called John Donnelly*, he's older and heavier than me, but every time we spar together, Uncle Richie tells me to take it easy on him. He's frightened John can't handle me.

The desire to win and the self-belief on the footy pitch is there from the start too, even when I play for De La Salle, my school team. If ever a player knocks me off the ball in a tackle I work on my strength training in the gym the following week. I promise myself that it won't happen again. No-one's going to beat me in a scrap for the ball.

If I look like losing my hunger, Dad pushes me a bit. When I play football on a Sunday afternoon, he always comes to watch. He encourages me to get stuck in. He gets more wound up than me sometimes. He tells me to work harder, to try more. I play one match and it's freezing, my hands are burning and my feet are like blocks of ice. I run over to the touchline.

'Here, Dad, I'm going to have to come off. It's too cold. I can't feel my feet.'

His face turns a funny colour and he looks like he's going to blow up with anger.

---

*John Donnelly, if you're wondering, is now a professional boxer, a super flyweight. I spent a lot of time thinking about becoming a pro fighter too, but in the end I went for football.

'What? You're cold?'

He can't believe it.

'Get out there and run more. Get on with it.'

I leg it around a bit harder to warm myself up. I'm only nine but I know that if Dad's advice is anything to go by, I'll have to toughen up even more if I want to be a proper footballer.

*****

All my heroes are battlers.

On the telly, I love watching boxers, especially Mike Tyson because his speed and aggression makes him so exciting. He always goes for the KO. When I watch Everton with Dad, my favourite player is Duncan Ferguson because he's a fighter like Iron Mike, hard as nails, and I love the way he never gives up, especially if things aren't going his way. He always gets stuck in. He also scores cracking goals. I could watch him play all day.

I love Everton, I'm mad for them. I write to the club and ask to become the mascot for a game when I'm 10 years old. A few weeks later a letter comes through the door telling me I've been chosen and I'm dead chuffed because I'm going to be walking out with the team for the Merseyside derby at Anfield. I step onto the pitch with our skipper, Dave Watson, and Liverpool's John Barnes and I can't believe the noise of the crowd. Later I go into the penalty area to take shots at our keeper, Neville Southall. I'm only supposed to be passing the ball back to him gently, but I get bored and chip one over his head and into the back of the net. I can see that he's not happy, so when he rolls the ball back to me, I chip him again.

I just want to score goals.

A couple of years later, I get to be a ball boy at Goodison Park. Neville's in goal again and as I run to get a shot that has gone out of play he starts shouting at me. 'Effin' hurry up, ball boy!' he yells. It scares the crap out of me. Afterwards, I go on about it for ages to my mates at school.

That afternoon at Anfield, Gary Speed scores for us, which I'm dead chuffed about because he's one of my favourite players. I can see that he works hard and he's a model pro. Someone tells me that he grew up as an Evertonian as well, so when my mum buys me a pet rabbit a little while later, I decide to name him 'Speedo'. Two days afterwards, the real Speedo signs for Newcastle and I'm moody for days.

*****

The training and the toughening up pays off.

I get spotted by club scouts when I'm nine years old and join Everton, which is like a dream come true. Then I play in the older teams at the club rather than my own age group because I'm technically better and physically stronger than the lads in my year. It's mad; I don't let on to the kids my age when I go to footy practice because I never play with them, I don't really know them. When I'm 14 years old, I work with the Everton Under-19s. Me, a kid, playing against (nearly) grown blokes and competing, scoring goals, winning tackles. It feels great.

It gets better. At 15, I play in the Everton reserves. At 16, I'm in the first team. I know I can play at this level because I'm grafting hard and a place in the side is my reward, just like Mum and Dad taught me. Some of the coaches wonder whether I've got enough strength to mix it with the pros, but I know I have bags of it because boxing with Uncle Richie has given me the muscle.

When we play Manchester United's reserves at our place, one of our coaches gives us instructions to be strong with Gary Neville, one of the stars of their first team. Everyone hates Gary Nev outside of Old Trafford because he's United through and through. He's always giving it on the pitch.

Not long into the game we both go up for a header. I accidentally catch him with my elbow and when I turn round to see if it's had any effect on him, he doesn't even flinch. The next time we go for a ball, he gets me back, clattering into me really hard.

It's just another lesson in playing the game.

$$*****$$

I don't change for 10 years. I take that same Crocky spirit onto the pitch throughout my career. Rolling up my sleeves, gritting my teeth and getting on with things helps me to a lot of goals at Manchester United. Like when I'm playing against Arsenal in January 2010. We're one-up through an own goal from their keeper, Manuel Almunia. Arsenal are one of our rivals for the Premier League and beating them will go some way to helping us win the title. I know that if we score again we'll probably take the game. Luckily, I manage to get us a second goal in the 37th minute, a strike that comes from not giving up.

I'm back defending, doing the dirty work, getting stuck in deep in the United half, which some strikers won't do. I win the ball on the edge of our penalty area, lay it off to Nani and leg it, checking the position of the Arsenal defence as I push on towards them. I can see their full-back, Gael Clichy, on one side of me, but I'm focused on Nani. He's bombing down the wing and I know a pass is coming my way if I can bust a gut to get into the right spot. He plays the ball into my path, I check my stride and thump a shot past Almunia first time which puts the result beyond Arsenal.

Three points in the bag.

When fans talk about the players with a desire to win games, they always mention the tacklers, the ball-winning midfielders, but desire to me is something different. It's my goal against Arsenal; it's sprinting for several seconds (again and again) to get onto a pass that might not come. Desire is playing out wide and making runs into the box and then tracking back to defend. Desire is risking injury to score. Desire is about trying your heart out and never giving up.

When the player stats came out for the Arsenal game – which they do for the Premier League every week – United's fitness coach, Tony Strudwick, comes into the dressing room at training with all the facts and figures. He reads out the speed of my run during the build up to our second goal. Apparently, I covered 60 metres in a ridiculous time.

'If you'd carried on running for another 40 metres at that pace, you'd have done the 100 metres in 9.4 seconds,' he says, looking at the flipchart with a smile on his face.

Everyone starts cracking up. That stat makes me quicker than Usain Bolt.

*****

Sometimes I go too far. The same blanked-out feeling that happens whenever I score takes over when the red mist comes down.

During an away game against Fulham in March 2009, nothing seems to go right for United and I lose it, big time. We've been beaten by Liverpool the week before and The Manager wants us to bounce back at Craven Cottage. Instead, we go a goal down after a penalty is given against Scholesy, who gets sent off for deliberately handling the ball in our box. I come on during the second half in place of Berbatov and pick up a booking.

I'm getting fouled all the time. With a minute left, the ball comes to me and somebody hacks at my ankles again, but the ref gives the decision to the other lot. I'm furious. I pick up the ball, meaning to luzz it to Jonny Evans, but I misjudge it and the ball flies hard past the ref.

He thinks I've thrown it at him.

Oh no, here we go.

Out comes the second yellow card, then the red. Game over.

I can only think of one thing.

This is going to cost us the league.

Two defeats on the bounce; a suspension for the next match. I'm livid. The red mist comes on. As I walk off the pitch, the crowd start to jeer. Everything boils up inside me, my head's banging. Sometimes in those situations, I get so angry that I never know what I'm going to do next. Thankfully, nobody gets in my way. The first thing that crosses my path is the corner flag. I lamp it. When I get to the dressing room, I punch the wall and nearly break my hand.

Paul Scholes is already sitting there, staring at me, just watching, as if it's only natural for me to stick a right hook onto a concrete wall. He's had time to shower and change. He's looking smart in his official club suit.

'You as well?'

I nod. My hand is killing me, I worry I might have busted it.

Nice one, Wayne.

Neither of us says a word. I sit there in my kit, fuming. Then a flash of fear comes into my head.

Oh god, The Manager's going to kill me.

I hear the final roar from the crowd as the whistle goes. We've lost, 2–0. I hear the players' studs clicking on the concrete path that leads to the dressing room. The door opens, but nobody talks as they sit down.

Silence.

Nobody looks at me. Giggsy, Jonny Evans, Rio, Edwin van der Sar, all of them stare at the floor. Then The Manager comes in and goes mad.

'You were poor as a team!' he screams. 'We didn't perform!'

He points at me, furious, red in the face, chewing gum.

'And you need to calm down. Relax!'

The Manager's right: I should relax, but he knows as well as me that the thought of losing is what drives me on in football, in everything, because he's built the same way.

We both hate to be second best.

*****

Look, I'm not always happy about it.

After the Fulham game, I worry that people have an opinion on what sort of person I am because of what they see on the football pitch. They see me punching corner flags and shouting on the telly and must think that I'm like that in everyday life. They watch me going in hard in the tackle and probably assume that I'm some kind of thug. Sometimes, when people see me pushing my son Kai around the supermarket with Coleen, they stare at me with their jaws open, like I should be in my kit, shinpads and boots, arguing with the bloke collecting the trollies, or kicking down a stack of toilet rolls in a massive strop.

These are much cheaper down the road!

I'm not like that though.

When I first meet people I'm quiet and shy. I don't open up that easily. I definitely don't react badly in conversation and I don't talk to friends and family in the same way as I talk to defenders and teammates. I don't tell them to 'eff off' if things don't go my way. I don't turn the computer off if I'm watching my pals play. Losing it only happens when I'm competing. And only if I lose. It's not something I'm proud of, but it's something I've had to live with. I obviously have two very different mindsets: one that drives me on in the thick of a game and another I live my life by. The two never cross over.

CHAPTER

2

HOME

Matches are won and lost in the tunnel at Old Trafford, but the one thing I notice when I stand there for the first time as a United player is that it seems to go on for miles and miles. It's long and dark. The ceilings are low and the players bump into one another as they walk to the pitch, almost shoulder to shoulder, because it's so narrow and cramped. At the end, over the heads of players, officials and the TV cameramen, past the red canopy that stretches out onto the pitch, I can see the bright green blur of the grass, the floodlights and the crowd and some United fans hanging over the edge of the wall, shouting and waving flags.

It's September 2004, United against Fenerbahçe. I'm about to make my first-team debut in the Champions League, a competition I've always dreamt of playing in.

The noise is mad, a buzz of 67,128 people, like a loud hum. When I first played here against United for Everton that buzz weighed me down a bit. It felt claustrophobic, it felt like a cup final. It did my head in. Now it pumps me up, but I can see why some players might feel trapped in here. Standing in the Old Trafford tunnel is like being in a box. If a footballer hasn't been here before and they're lined up next to the United players for the first time, it's a terrifying moment. The weight of expectation is huge. A player has to be able to handle it if they're going to be able to play well in front of the crowd here.

The Manager knows all about the importance of this place. The atmosphere is such a big deal that he even makes it his business to find out which players from the opposition have faced us here before and which ones haven't. He tells us before a game; he knows who's frightened and he wants us to know, too. Sometimes, as we get ready he lists names from the other lot, the lads playing here for the first time – they're the ones who might not be on their game.

Later in the season I see it for myself. In some teams, the newly promoted ones usually, the players look scared as they start their walk to the pitch. Others look as if they're starting their big day out for the season, or even their career. I can tell that they want to make the most of it, that they want to soak up the occasion. They clock their families in the stands and smile and wave like it's their biggest ever achievement. As they make the slow walk from the tunnel in the corner of the ground to the halfway line they're thinking one thing: *Bloody hell, this is Old Trafford*. Good news for us:

the distraction can stop them from thieving a point. Bad news for them: they're 1–0 down psychologically.

Now I'm about to make my first walk from the tunnel in a United shirt.

Today it's all about my signing, my first game. I've been at the club nearly two months, but I haven't played a minute of first team football after I busted a bone in my foot at Euro 2004, which has been annoying for everyone because I cost the club a lot of money. Still, the fans have been sound. I see them on the box and they're saying how excited they are to see me here, but the one worry at the back of my mind is that it might take a while for them to accept me because I'm a Scouser. I might have to do something really special to win them over.

They're on my side tonight, though. The crowd are singing my name before I even get onto the pitch.

'Rooney!'
'Rooney!'
'Roooooooo-neeeeee!'

The shivers run down my spine as I walk into the glare of the floodlights for the first time in a red shirt. I'm bricking it.

It makes me laugh whenever I watch the tape of that game now: I come out of the tunnel with a chewy in my mouth and my eyes don't seem to move as I walk across the grass. I don't even blink. I stare straight ahead, trying to focus. The camera catches me puffing my chest out, getting myself ready, staring at the sky above the massive stand in front of me. I don't look at anything in particular, just a space above that huge wall of people which seems to stretch up forever, full of red and black and white and some yellow and green.

I want to soak up the noise.

I don't want to turn round.

I don't want to see how massive everything looks.

Bloody hell, this is Old Trafford.

*****

Everything had been so quiet and calm before.

I sat in the dressing room ahead of the game and watched as everybody prepared themselves. I saw some of the biggest names in the league getting ready: winger Ryan Giggs stretching his skinny frame, Gary Neville bouncing on the spot; Dutch striker Ruud van Nistelrooy and Rio Ferdinand playing two touch with a ball, their passes pinging off the concrete floor. It was totally different to the atmosphere at Everton.

At Goodison it was rowdy and loud, people shouted, yelled, issued instructions. It dawned on me that some teams have to win games through team spirit; they have to fight harder for one another. Pumping up the dressing room builds a strong attitude. It helps to psyche out the opposition. Before the Fenerbahçe game I noticed that everyone in a United shirt prepared in their own way – calmly, quietly. No one screamed or shouted. They knew that if we played well we'd win the game no problem. There was no need to scream and shout.

I felt like I'd come to the right place.

*****

I make a good early pass. Well, I take the kick-off so I can't really mess that one up. My first proper touch comes a few moments later and I play that one well, too. I'm running on pure adrenaline.

I want to impress everyone. I want to show them what I can do.

Then, in the 17th minute I score my first-ever United goal.

Ruud plays me through. I'm one-on-one with the goalie and everything slows down – the weirdest feeling in football. It seems to take an hour before I get to the penalty area, as if I'm running in really thick mud. My brain goes into overdrive like it always does in this situation, as if it's a computer working out all the sums needed to score a goal.

Is the keeper off his line?

Is a defender closing in on me?

Should I take it round the goalie?

Should I shoot early?

Will I look a divvy if I try to 'meg him and I hit the ball wide?

A one-on-one like this is probably the hardest thing to pull off in a game because there's too much time to process all the info, too much time to think. Too much time to over-complicate what should be an easy job.

I'm just going to put my foot through it, see what happens.

I hit the ball with all my strength and it rockets into the back of the net. Old Trafford goes nuts. Right now I doubt anyone cares whether I'm a Scouser or not, I'm off the mark. Mentally I loosen up, I feel like I can express myself a little bit, try a few things. Not long afterwards, Ryan Giggs plays a ball across to me. I drop a shoulder, do my defender and fire the ball into the bottom corner. Now the crowd are singing my name again; now I'm daring to dream.

What would it be like to score a hat-trick at Old Trafford?

I find out in the second half. There's a free-kick on the edge of the Fenerbahçe area and Giggsy, with all his amazing ability and experience, puts the ball down to take it, but I want it. I've got bucketloads of confidence and I fancy my chances, just like I did whenever I got into the ring with a bigger lad in Uncle Richie's boxing gym. I just know I'm going to score – it's mad, I can almost sense it's going to happen.

'Giggsy, I'm putting this one away.'

He hands the ball over and I curl a shot into the top left-hand corner, easy as you like. Goal number three, a hat-trick on my Old Trafford debut.

We win 6–2 and in the dressing room afterwards every-one seems to be in a state of shock. I don't think anybody can believe what I've just done out there. I can't get my brain around it either. Rio sits there shaking his head, looking at me like I've just landed from outer space. The older lads, like Gary Nev and Giggsy, are thinking the same thing, I can tell, but they're keeping it in. They've probably seen amazing stuff like this loads of times before with players like Eric Cantona and David Beckham, so they stay silent. They probably don't want to build me up just yet. To them, my hat-trick is part of another day at the office, just like it is to The Manager, who shakes my hand and tells me I've made a good start to my United career.

Nobody's getting carried away.

There isn't a massive party to enjoy afterwards, no one gets bevvied up or hits the town. Some players I know would be out with their teammates having scored a hat-trick on their debut. Instead, everyone goes home. But not me, I haven't even got a gaff to go to. Coleen and I are living out of a hotel while we look for a new house, so to celebrate the start of my Old Trafford career we order room service and watch the match highlights on the box, but it all seems so weird.

I feel numb.

I always knew that I was going to experience a massive change in my life by signing for United, but I didn't expect it to be this big. The strangest thing is, I don't feel like I'm on the verge of anything special. I don't feel like a special player. I've never felt that way, even as a kid playing for Everton. Tonight as we sit eating our room service tea I feel confident, confident that I have the ability to help United win games and trophies, but I can see that everyone else in the dressing room has the ability to do that, too.

At Old Trafford I'm nothing special; I'm not a standout player. But I reckon I can help United to be a standout team.

*****

Despite my brilliant start, it doesn't take long for me to get up Roy Keane's nose.

On the pitch, Roy's a leader; I can see that from training with him. He yells a lot, he inspires through example, but he rarely dishes out instructions – he's just really demanding, always telling us to graft harder.

He can be just as demanding off the pitch.

On the night before my first away game against Birmingham City (a 0–0 draw), the squad sits down for tea in the team hotel, a fancy place with a private dining room just for us, complete with plasma screen telly. Roy's watching the rugby, but the minute he gets up to go to the loo, I swipe the controls and flip the channel so the lads can watch *The X Factor* on the other side. Then I stuff the remote in my trackie pocket.

When Roy comes back and notices Simon Cowell's face on the telly, he's not happy. He starts shouting.

'Who's turned it over? Where's the remote?'

I don't say a word. Nobody does. Everyone starts looking around the room, trying to avoid his glare.

'Well, if no one's watching this, I'll turn it off.'

Roy walks up to the telly and yanks the plug out of the wall. The lads sit there in silence. There isn't a sound, apart from the scrape of cutlery on plates. It's moody.

After dinner we all crash out early, but at around midnight, I get a knock on the door. It's the club security guard.

'Alright Wayne,' he says. 'Roy's sent me. He wants to know where the remote controls are.'

I realise it's Roy's way of letting on to me that he knows exactly what's happened. It's a message.

You're for it now.

I hand them over and wonder what's going to happen. But the next day he says nothing about it.

*****

When I first sign for United, I think back to the times I'd watched them winning trophies and league titles on the telly. It happened a lot. I'd see their ex-players being interviewed on *Sky Sports News* or *Football Focus* and whenever their names came up on the screen it would always read: 'Steve Bruce: Premier League Winner', or 'Teddy Sheringham: Treble Winner.'

I want that to be me.

Later, when I train at Carrington for the first time, Gary Neville gives me some advice. He says, 'The thing with this team is, no matter how much you've achieved, no matter how many medals you've won, you're never allowed to think that you've made it.'

I'm a bit nervous about meeting Gary Neville again. I'd whacked him during that reserve game after all – I worry that he'll remember it. It doesn't help that just before my arrival one of the papers runs a story about Gary hating Scousers. Apparently he's told a reporter, 'I can't stand Liverpool, I can't stand Liverpool people, I can't stand anything about them.' I'm a bit worried that me and him won't get on.

41

I ask him whether he's really said it, whether he really hates Scousers. He tells me it's rubbish – he'd been chatting about the Liverpool side of the '80s. He'd grown up watching them win trophy after trophy. He hated their team; he wasn't having a pop at the people in the city, just the club. That's good enough for me. As an Evertonian I can see his point.

I like Gary straightaway, he's a funny lad. We warm up together in training by playing keep ball in one of the boxes marked out on the training ground turf. I spoon the ball and give a pass away. From behind me I hear him winding me up. 'Flippin' heck, how much did we pay for Wazza?'

At lunch after the practice game, he doesn't stop talking, he goes on and on and on, but in a nice way. Sometimes when he's off on one – about music, his guitar playing, football – it's as if he doesn't have the time to stop for breath, especially if he's talking about United. He's the most passionate player I've ever met. He's hard too, on the pitch and off it. He gets stuck into tackles; in the dressing room I notice that The Manager has a go at Gaz probably more than any of the other players in the team because he can handle it. He isn't soft like some footballers can be.

When he's out there playing, he's the spirit of The Manager. He carries that same ambition to win, that same desire. There's one game where I sit on the bench with him and he even acts like The Manager. He watches the way our match unfolds and he studies the tactics of the opposition. Then with 20 minutes to go he sends a youth team player out to warm up on the touchlines for a laugh without The Manager knowing. Talk about cheek.

Gary and players like Paul Scholes and Ryan Giggs bring a lot of experience to the dressing room. In my first few months at the club there are times when teams who can't live with us on paper defend for their lives and nearly get away with it, even at Old Trafford. They hassle us and battle for every tackle; they park the team bus in front of their goal every time we win back possession. I get frustrated. I lose my patience and start hitting risky long balls and taking pot shots in a desperate attempt to win the game, but Gary calms me down.

'Keep trying, Wazza, keep playing. A chance will come.'

Nine times out of ten, he's right.

I'm not the only one to hear the advice. There's a young lad called Ronaldo who signed a season earlier from Sporting Lisbon for a cool £12.2 million, and everyone starts talking about how he's going to be the future of the club alongside me. There's nothing on him though: he's a bag of tricks, but he's skinny. He's got braces on his teeth, slicked hair and he's spotty. Ronaldo looks like a boy. It's hard to believe we're around the same age.

Wonder how he's going to turn out?

*****

As I get settled at the club, the size of United amazes me. I watch the news at home and no matter where the cameras are, the Middle East, somewhere in Africa, wherever, there's always a little kid wearing an old United shirt. At first it freaks me out, but then fame always has done.

The first time I'd heard that fans were going into the Everton club shop for my shirt, it felt weird. It used to confuse me when people wanted my autograph in the street. I was 14 when it happened for the first time, playing a youth team game for Everton. When the final whistle went, a bloke came up to me and asked for my signature.

'I'm going to keep this because when you grow up it's going to be worth a lot of money,' he says.

Seeing myself on the box was even weirder.

I played in both legs of the FA Youth Cup final in 2002 against Aston Villa and picked up the Man of the Match award afterwards, even though we lost. Sky interviewed me for the show after one game and I watched it back when I got home because my mum had videoed it. I hated it when I saw the clip: it didn't look like me, it didn't sound like me. It was weird.

At United I realise straightaway that the attention is much more intense and the players are treated like rock stars. It's scary because the team has fans everywhere and people recognise me wherever I go. In the street, blokes, mums and kids come up to me for autographs, and most of the time I'm comfortable with it, but there are moments when it gets too much. I'm only 18 years old; it's difficult to deal with the attention sometimes.

Every time I go shopping I see a picture of myself in the papers the next day; one night I go out for a meal and people point and stare when I'm sitting with my family. It's like I'm a waxwork from Madame Tussauds rather than a person. A party of people starts telling the family on the next table that 'it's that Wayne Rooney over there'. Then they start pointing and taking pictures with their phones on the sly. In the shops I'm happy to sign stuff, pose for photos and talk to people, but it's a bit much when I'm eating my tea.

I decide I'm not going to bang on about fame to my mates or moan about it to the lads at the club though, because that's what so many other footballers do. Signing for United means I have to deal with this situation. It's part of my job, but I realise I'm growing up fast. I'm learning how to live my life under a mad spotlight.

One afternoon, shortly after the Fenerbahçe game, I go to the garage to fill the car up. As I put the petrol in, a bloke pulls up next to me and winds his window down.

'Here, Wayne, you fill up your own car yourself, do you?'

Like anyone else is going to do it.

CHAPTER 3
CARRINGTON

The Manager's office is right in the thick of things at Carrington, United's training ground, upstairs from the changing rooms, next to the canteen. If someone was to wander into the club at lunch on a Monday without checking the footy results first, they'd know exactly how United have got on just by taking a look at The Manager's body language. As he buzzes around the dining tables at lunch, having a crack with people, chatting, joking (or not chatting, not joking), it's written all over his face.

If we've won, like against Fenerbahçe, he laughs with everyone; he talks about the last game and gets excited about the next. If we've been playing really well, he tells unfunny jokes and shouts out silly trivia questions while we eat our lunch or get changed.

'Lads, name the current players from the Premier League with a World Cup winners' medal?' he says.

He keeps us guessing for ages. I don't think he actually knows the answers half the time. If he does, he never gives them to us when we pester him afterwards.

When he's in a really good mood, the stories start. He goes on about his playing career and the goals he scored as a striker for Dunfermline and Rangers. He tells the tale about the time he once played with a broken back. Apparently everyone in the squad's heard it – how bad the pain was, how he got the injury. The Manager tells the 'Broke Back' tale so many times that it's not long before I know it from beginning to end. But it doesn't stop him from telling it again, especially when he feels there's a point to be made about injuries. The funny thing is, even though he talks about his playing days a lot, I've never seen any video evidence of his goals, so I don't know how good or not good he was. I doubt he was as great as he makes out.

In my first few months at the club, I realise that when the atmosphere around Carrington is good – when we're winning – I can go into The Manager's office whenever I want, just for a chat. To be honest, I like going in there. It's a big room, bigger than some dressing rooms I've been in. A huge window overlooks the training pitches so he can see just about everything that's going on.

'Wayne, the door is always open if you need to speak to me,' he says.

When I go in there for the first time, shortly after my debut, we talk about the game, our upcoming opponents, how I should play to exploit their weaknesses. We talk about the title race and the league's best players: Chelsea are strong he reckons, Arsenal and Liverpool, too. He tells me how he sees our team shaping up, how me and Ronaldo are going to do. We talk about horses, he tells me about his wine collection – apparently he has a big cellar at home. He doesn't mention retirement, even though he's at an age when most people would be happy to put their feet up, but that's the measure of the man, I suppose.

I feel I can have a laugh with him as we're playing well. I even make out that I already know the team for our next match, days before he's announced it.

'Who's playing up front with me, boss? Am I playing up top on my own?'

He laughs. 'Oh, so you think you're playing, do you? Who else is in the team then?'

I rattle off a few names.

'Yeah, well, you're not too far off.'

As the season progresses, I discover that the only time I don't like going in there is when I've been called up to see him. That usually means he's unhappy with something I'm doing, or not doing, and it always happens when training has finished for the day. There's a telephone in the players' changing room. When it starts to ring, the lads know what's coming next: a summons from The Manager. Someone's going to get it.

'Can you send Wayne to my office, please?'

When it's me, the lads make funny noises, like I'm going to be in loads of trouble. Some of them make a sharp intake of breath, or whistle, just to wind me up.

Like the time in January 2005 when we're preparing to play Liverpool. He makes the phone call. When I go into his office and sit on the big settee, he tells me I'm not playing well enough. He tells me I haven't been thinking properly on the pitch.

'You've got to start concentrating more, Wayne,' he says. 'I want you to keep things simple. You're going out wide too much and I want you to stay up in the penalty area.'

I argue. I think it's an unfair assumption of my game, but I accept his advice and get on with it. At Anfield I stay in the box as much as I can, I don't drift wide. Then I answer him in the best way possible: I score the winning goal. Maybe that was his plan all along. Maybe he wanted to wind me up.

After a defeat, The Manager's mood can be quite dark; he doesn't talk to the players or joke around for a couple of weeks. He speaks to us as a group in team talks, but that's as far as it goes. If anyone passes him at the training ground, he doesn't say a word to them. I learn pretty quickly that it's best to stay out of his way after a bad result. In my first few months at the club, when I see him eating in the canteen after a defeat, I steer clear. I get my food, keep my head down and walk to my table as quickly as I can.

*****

There's one thought I can't shake: the first time I was introduced to The Manager properly was when I signed for United at Old Trafford in the summer of 2004. I'd spoken to him once or twice when Everton played United – a quick hello in the tunnel, but that was it. The day I joined the club, I met him at Carrington and I was dead excited.

He drove me to Old Trafford and told me how I was going to fit into the team and how he wanted me to play. He told me about my new teammates: winger Ryan Giggs, England internationals Rio Ferdinand, Paul Scholes and Gary Neville; my new strike partner, Ruud van Nistelrooy – a goal machine.

I talked about the times I'd played at Old Trafford for Everton, how I'd been blown away by the atmosphere there. I'd even said to my dad afterwards, 'I want to play for them one day.'

It was surreal. I'd been watching him on the telly for years with players like Eric Cantona and David Beckham, but I never imagined that it would happen to me. Later, when word got around back home about my day, a mate sent a text over.

'BLOODY HELL!!!' he said. 'CAN'T BELIEVE U'VE GOT FERGIE CHAUFFEURING U AROUND.'

The Manager seemed like a really good bloke, but the next day I experienced his legendary influence first hand. It was a nice afternoon, so I drove over to Crocky to see the family. On the way, I spotted Mum and Dad in the car park of the local pub and I pulled over to say hello. We decided to go in for a drink, a diet pop for me. I was only there for 10 or 15 minutes before I went home, but a day later, The Manager called me into his office. My first summons.

'Wayne, what were you doing in that pub in Croxteth yesterday?' he said.

I couldn't believe it. I'd not been in there long, but long enough for someone to make a phone call and grass me up. To this day I still don't know who did it. I left the meeting knowing one thing, though: *The Manager has eyes and ears everywhere.*

Within weeks I know plenty more stuff. He has an amazing knowledge of the game. When we play teams, he knows everything about the opposition, and I mean everything. If a player has a weakness on his right foot, he knows about it. If one full-back is soft in the air, he'll have identified him as a potential area of attack. He also knows the strengths of every single player in the other team's squad. Before games we're briefed on who does what and where. He also warns us of the players we should be extra wary of.

His eye for detail is greater than anyone else's I've ever worked with, but that's one of the reasons why I signed for him. That and the fact that he's won everything in the game:

The Premier League.
The FA Cup.
The League Cup.
The Community Shield.
The Champions League.
The UEFA Cup Winners' Cup.
The UEFA Super Cup.
The World Club Championship.
The Intercontinental Cup.

You can't argue with a trophy cabinet like that.

*****

I start my first league game for United against Boro' in October and we begin the game badly. By now I've learned that The Manager expects one thing from us when we play: to win.

After half an hour, we're a goal down and unable to get a foothold in the game. I'm not playing well and he's shouting at me from the dugout. I pretend not to hear him. I don't turn around, I don't want to make eye contact. I know he's shouting, but I can't really make out what he's saying because the crowd's so loud. I definitely don't want to get up close enough to hear him because I know it'll be scary.

He looks terrifying on the touchline.

We eventually draw 1–1 against Boro' but The Manager isn't happy. It's a game we should have won and in my first few months at United I learn quickly that we have to attack until the end of a game, no matter what the score is. That's The Manager's football philosophy. He tells us that he wants the players to get behind the ball when we're defending and move with speed when we're attacking. He wants us to draw the opposition in, to lull them into a false sense of security. 'That's when they'll start stringing passes together, growing in confidence,' he tells us. 'But it's a trap.'

That's when we're supposed to win the ball back and punish the other lot with some quick passes through midfield. 'The opposition won't stand a chance,' he says.

The ball needs to be fired out wide and hit into the box to me and Ruud. My role in all of this is to make good runs in behind the defence. When the ball comes to me in deeper areas I'm supposed to hold it up and bring other players into the game, like Ronaldo. When the ball gets played out wide I have to head for the box and get on the end of crosses.

If we play well, Carrington is a happy place. After Fenerbahçe, The Manager allows us to enjoy our training. We watch videos of all the things we've done well in a game and he tells us to continue playing the way we are. He wants us to keep up our winning momentum. If we can do that, the canteen is a happier spot for everyone.

CHAPTER

4

PAYBACK

Arsenal, 24 October 2004.

Needle match.

It's a needle match because Arsenal have been title rivals with United for over a decade. The two teams have had some pretty tasty games with one another in the past and there have been rucks, 20-man scraps and red cards.

The worst game took place the previous season when it kicked off between both sets of players. As I watched the game on the telly after playing for Everton, a row started between Ruud and some of the Arsenal lads – the type of fight fans always love watching. It began when striker Diego Forlan won a penalty; the Arsenal lot began complaining that he'd dived for it and when Ruud then spooned his spot-kick, a mob of their players crowded around him and got in his face, winding him up. They were angry because they thought he had got their skipper, Patrick Viera, sent off earlier in the game, but the reaction was horrible. Martin Keown was the worst; he screamed at Ruud and jumped up and down like a right head case. His eyes nearly popped out. He looked like a zombie from a horror film.

Now it's my turn to be in the thick of one of the biggest battles in the Premier League.

In the build up there's loads of talk about the atmosphere of the match around town; the papers are going on about the previous season's clash and I can't turn on the telly without seeing *that* scuffle between Ruud and Keown. It's obviously bothering Ruud because he's been quiet for days. There's an atmosphere about him. He's withdrawn and he doesn't talk to the other lads in the dressing room at Carrington as much.

In the short time I've known Ruud he's always looked focused, but this week there's something else going on inside his head, something driving him on. No one asks him about the game or his mood, but I can tell that he wants to prove a point. I reckon that his penalty miss against Arsenal must have weighed on him for months.

When it comes to the match, both teams are up for it – the Arsenal players even hug one another before the game, like they're getting ready to go into a battle – and once the footy gets underway the atmosphere at Old Trafford is horrible, moody, because the two sides are at one another's throats. It's my 19th birthday, but nobody's dishing out any prezzies on the pitch.

The game is evenly matched, though. We're at home and looking to kick-start our season again after those disappointing draws against Birmingham and Boro'; Arsenal are on a 49-game unbeaten streak and they're a great team – Dennis Bergkamp, Ashley Cole, Thierry Henry and Patrick Vieira are all playing and they're on top of their game, but the thing is they know it. All week they've been banging on about how great it will be to make it to 50 games undefeated at Old Trafford.

Big mistake. They've fired us up.

Fifty games unbeaten? No way. Not at our place.

Already I know that this is the way a footballer has to think if they're to do well at United.

Nobody gets to believe that we're a pushover.

The tackles fly in thick and fast from the start, every loose ball matters. After a tight first half, we go in at the break goalless, then in the second, Ruud gets a chance to make up for last year's penalty miss when on 73 minutes I burst into the area. Sol Campbell makes a fair tackle and nicks the ball but his momentum brings me down. He decks me. I hear a whistle and I know straightaway that the ref is pointing to the spot because the crowd are going nuts and Ashley Cole and Sol are complaining, shouting that I've dived, that I've not been tripped. The funny thing is, they're both right and wrong: I haven't been fouled, but I haven't dived either. Instead, there's been a coming together and it's given the ref a decision to make. Thankfully for us he gives the penalty.

Everyone starts looking to Ruud, who's already got the ball in his hands. I know I'm not going to get a look-in when it comes to taking this pen because he wants it badly and everyone's willing him on to score, like it's payback time. It feels like the whole of Old Trafford is wishing the ball into the net, but as I watch, Ruud doesn't seem to be setting himself up right. I've seen him practising pens in training every day and he always goes the same way. He hits his shot hard and the keeper usually has no chance. When he steps up to the spot this time, he changes his usual direction and strikes the ball poorly. Straightaway I know that if Arsenal's goalie, Jens Lehmann, guesses right he's going to save the shot because there's not enough pace on it.

I think he's fluffed it.

Ruud's 'mare is going to get even worse. Everything seems to stop still. But then Lehmann reads it wrong. He throws himself in the opposite direction and as Ruud's shot hits the back of the net the whole place erupts and he's off, running to the fans. He's not looking to his teammates or the bench or The Manager, but I can see there's joy and relief all over his face. It's probably the most genuine emotion I've ever seen in a footballer after scoring – it's like Ruud has had the weight of the world lifted off his shoulders.

I chase after him as he runs to the corner flag and drops to his knees, head back. He's screaming, his fists are clenched. I think of Stuart Pearce when he scored for England against Spain in Euro 96 during a penalty shootout in the quarter-finals. He went mental, the memory of one blobbed penalty against West Germany in the 1990 World Cup semis wiped off with a single kick of the ball.

Now it's the same for Ruud.

It's pure emotion.

I want to celebrate too, but I can see by the way he's looking up at the sky, soaking up the huge Old Trafford roar, that he needs this moment to himself. Fair play to him, he deserves it.

The Arsenal lot look absolutely gutted, and now we're a goal to the good I know we'll stop them from getting that 50th undefeated result. The thought of it pushes the team on for the last 15 minutes and we defend strongly while pressing for a second on the break. Then in the 90th minute I put the final nail into Arsenal's coffin.

Our midfielder, Alan Smith – Yorkshire lad, bleached blond hair – gets the ball out wide; I make a run into the box when his pass comes over. As I leg it for the ball an Arsenal defender starts kicking at my heels. It's Lauren, he's trying to trip me, but I'm not going down. I want my first league goal for United so badly that I manage to keep my balance. It leaves me with a tap-in to score.

Ta, very much. 2–0.

My first Premier League strike for United.

'Happy birthday to me.'

*****

When the final whistle blows shortly afterwards, I walk to the dressing room and strip off my kit. There's only a few of us in here, everyone else is still coming down the tunnel. My shirt and shorts are off, my socks around my ankles. I'm thinking about getting a shower when all of a sudden I hear shouting, loads of it. I look out of the door and our lot are going toe to toe with Arsenal's players, pushing, shoving, everyone getting in one another's faces. It's all scrappy stuff, no one's lamping anyone, it just looks like one of those mass brawls that sometimes kick off in a game of football. It's handbags stuff.

Arsenal obviously can't handle it. They don't like the unbeaten run coming to an end, especially at Old Trafford, and especially with all the history between the two teams. I think the fact that Ruud has scored today hacks them off even more.

After a few moments, everything calms down and the lads get back to the dressing room to soak up the victory again. But then The Manager walks in. He looks shocked. He's wearing a different top to the one he had on during the game, which is weird.

One of our lads says, 'Somebody threw a pizza at The Manager.'

I look at him. We've won, but he's not walking around, shaking everyone by the hand like he usually does. He seems unsettled, which is something I thought I'd never see.

Everyone gets back to talking about the game.

We've stopped Arsenal from making it to 50 games unbeaten.

We've won 2–0; Ruud has scored.

We look at the Premier League table:

PREMIER LEAGUE TABLE, 24 OCTOBER 2004

	PLAYED	GD	POINTS
1/ ARSENAL	10	19	25
2/ CHELSEA	10	10	23
3/ EVERTON	10	4	22
4/ BOLTON	10	4	18
5/ UNITED	10	4	17

We've got a great result against the league leaders, we're within touching distance of the top teams and maybe the result will launch our season. But the atmosphere in the dressing room feels a little bit weird.

*****

After Arsenal, we fall on our backsides by losing 2–0 to Portsmouth at Fratton Park. Then we go on a five-month unbeaten league run, defeating Arsenal again, Palace, City, Liverpool and Villa along the way. It's not until the beginning of April that we get beaten, 2–0 by Norwich. Then comes the game I've been waiting for all season: Everton away, Goodison Park.

Time to face the music.

It's the first time I've played here since signing at Old Trafford and I know the Everton fans aren't exactly made up about me playing for United. In fact, they hate it. When the transfer was going through in the summer, death threats were sent to the house. I even had to get personal security sorted out for my mum and dad.

I know exactly what to expect as the United bus winds its way through the backstreets that lead to the ground because I've driven this way loads of times before as a player. I've even walked this route as a fan when I watched the games with my dad or travelled to the ground as a ball boy. I reckon there's going to be a crowd of hundreds waiting to give the away team some stick as we get off the bus.

We turn the corner.

I can see the police horses and the burger vans.

Goodison comes into view, then the crowds waiting for us. For me.

Bloody hell, there's thousands of them.

The mob are waiting by the club gates, dozens deep, all of them booing as the team coach turns into the car park. Everyone onboard knows they're here to have a pop at me, so they start pulling my leg, winding me up. Someone makes a joke about my mates waiting to say hello, but then a brick bounces off the side of the bus. Then another. I hear the horrible pop of breaking glass. Someone's thrown a bottle. I sussed I'd be getting some stick this afternoon, but nothing has prepared me for this. As the bus door opens, I make the short walk down the steps in full view of the Everton fans. They're seeing me in a United suit for the first time and the boos and jeers are deafening.

It's pure anger.

The atmosphere is upsetting. Everton are the team I've grown up supporting and although I'm with United now, I still want them to do well. OK, not today, but they're the side I played for and dreamt of playing for when I was a little kid. To get abuse from people who I've probably stood side by side with in the stands really hurts. They're fans of a club that's still close to my heart.

Then I walk into the ground and everything feels strange.

It's the same building, with the same faces and the same fittings, but the atmosphere is disorientating. I'm in the place where I grew up, the stadium where I made my name as a footballer, but it feels alien. Sitting in the away dressing room at Goodison Park doesn't seem right.

But I'm not going to let it throw me.

I get my head straight. *Focus.* The Everton fans out there haven't intimidated me, they've made me even more desperate to win. I want to score. I want to show them what I'm really capable of. *I want to shut them up.* There are some footballers I know who would happily take a draw when they play their former clubs, but I'm not like that. Today, I want to win so badly.

When I line up in the tunnel during the minutes before the game, I can tell that the home supporters are really up for it today. I hear the theme from *Z-Cars*, the club's anthem, as the two teams move towards the pitch. When I walk out of the tunnel into the sunlight and see the Gwladys Street End, the boos are deafening. All of them are aimed at me and the hairs on the back of my neck start to tingle. Now I'm really wound up. Any thoughts of being an Everton fan disappear on the spot.

I have to score today.

When the whistle goes for the kick-off, the expected happens: my first touch is greeted with thousands and thousands of boos. As is the next one. And the next. And the next. I hold my temper and we hold our own for the first 45 minutes, but the second half turns into a 'mare for all of us. Everton are pumped up with that cup final feeling, they fight all over the pitch. Duncan Ferguson, my hero as a school kid, scores in the 55th minute. Gary Nev boots a ball into the fans and gets a straight red, then in injury time Scholesy gets sent off after a second yellow.

When I walk off the park at full-time with the game lost, the laughter and the cheering from the Everton fans sound louder than boos.

It's the worst part of the day.

*****

Some goals feel more important than others. Scoring the fourth in a 4–1 win is nice, but not special. Scoring a consolation goal in a 3–1 defeat means nothing. Hat-tricks are always amazing.

Scoring an absolute screamer is even better, probably because it all happens in a split second, so it's always surprising.

In April, I hit a blinder against Newcastle at home. A volley from about 25 yards that leaves my boot and rifles over Shay Given in the Newcastle goal. The funny thing is, as it happens, I'm arguing with the ref. We've just won a free-kick and Alan Shearer has booted the ball away. I'm trying to get him booked. I'm even more moody because we're losing 1–0 after a Darren Ambrose goal and I've picked up a dead leg. The Manager wants to bring me off.

As play restarts, the ball is played upfield. I follow it, still chewing the ref's ear off, but I stop short of the box. The ball gets headed out from the Newcastle defence and drops right in front of me at the perfect height. Out of anger, I smack it as hard as I can and it flies right into the top corner like a rocket. Old Trafford goes mental.

Dead leg? What dead leg?

CHAPTER

5

GRAFT

Every day at work begins with the same drive into Carrington, past the autograph hunters waiting at the gates with their shirts, posters and old matchday programmes. I pull into the car park with the Beemers and the Mercs. The Manager's Audi is here – he's in work hours before anyone else at the club and he's probably the last to leave at night. It doesn't matter what time I turn up or what time I leave, The Manager's car is always parked in the same spot.

I walk through the club reception with its fancy model of Old Trafford in the foyer and down a brightly lit corridor. Along the way I pass the photos on the wall: the famous Busby Babes; Giggsy and Ronaldo celebrating a goal; The Manager looking scary in a smart suit.

Down the corridor, through more doors into the dressing room. I can hear some of the lads in there already, laughing. Gary Neville, Darren Fletcher, Rio, Wes Brown.

'Alright, Wazza?'

I say hello and get my kit ready. The United squad meet here before every training session. You can tell because it looks like a kid's bedroom. There's rubbish on the floor – Ribena cartons, cycling magazines and the cardboard packaging from a new pair of shinpads – alongside trainers, flip flops, towels. On the wall there's a TV screen. It tells the players when they're due to have a pedicure or massage; the lunch menu is always up there. Somebody's stuck a toy monkey on one of the shelves. There's an iPod dock so we can play tunes.

My locker's in the corner. On the door, someone's cheekily stuck an old magazine cutting of me and Coleen from a couple of years ago. Sometimes when I'm sitting in here, getting changed, I can't believe my luck.

I'm a professional footballer.

It's great playing football every day for a living. Sometimes I hear of players who don't like training, but I love it. I mean, what's not to like? The rules are pretty simple: be in for 9.30; anyone who's late gets fined. Once we're in work, do what The Manager says. It's a doddle.

Today we go through the usual routine. We get ready and the lads have a laugh and mess around. Then we take our first warm-up session: a gentle, 20-minute cycle on the exercise bikes.

We get our footy boots and go outside.

We play keep ball in a box marked on the training ground and eight of us flick the ball around while two players in the middle try to pinch it back. This drill gets us used to the ball. Afterwards we do short, sharp sprints between a set of cones to get our lungs and legs going.

Then it's the part of the day I love most: the practice game.

I never know what type of game we're going to be doing from day to day. Sometimes we work on possession, other times we work on tactics. Today we look at how we're going to break down the opposition in our next match: Charlton Athletic. While this goes on, The Manager stands on the sidelines, watching us play. He tells us to increase the tempo if we need to. He tells us to get the ball into the box quicker. He changes us positionally.

In the practice match, everyone wants to win, even a game like this eight-a-side today. The tackles fly in, thick and fast.

Wes Brown comes in late on me, his foot well over the ball. He cracks me on the ankle. I'm in the area, but the ref, our fitness coach, doesn't give anything. My team start moaning, I'm livid. Moments later, in the same spot, Wes catches me again. It's high. His studs are showing and it's a blatant foul, but still there's no sign of us getting a penalty. Then he runs up the other end and scores.

The Manager watches from the sidelines. All of a sudden he stops the game.

'Lads, calm down! Watch the tackles. I don't want anyone getting injured.'

The next time I run into the penalty area, I feel a slight touch and decide to dive (we all do in training).

That's got to be a pen!

Nothing's given.

Now I'm furious.

I start shouting at the ref because I want to win this game as much as I want to win a Premier League game against City or Chelsea, or Aston Villa. There's an argument, like there is nearly every day in training, but it's par for the course. The battling atmosphere, that edge, comes from The Manager – he wants us to train like we're playing for real.

The ref blows his whistle.

Game over.

I'm furious because we've lost, but I carry on shooting, firing balls towards a goal for ten minutes. It's all part of the routine: I'm getting ready for any opportunity that might come my way at the weekend.

I hit volleys.

I hit shots from outside the box.

I hit shots where I have to control a ball passed into my chest.

I hit penalties, free-kicks.

Then one of our coaches makes me stand with my back turned away from the ball. He rolls a pass across the box in a random direction and then calls out to me. I turn, react, and shoot as quickly as I can. It gets me ready for those loose balls in the 18-yard area – I want to be prepared for anything.

I'm not the only one. When I look around the training ground afterwards, I see different players working on different drills. Rio on headers, our keeper Tim Howard on crosses, Giggsy on free-kicks.

We can all improve in one way or another, even at United.

*****

People always go on about the art of goalscoring and whether it comes down to natural ability or training, but to be honest, I reckon goals come from a combination of both. Some of it can be coached, but you can't teach instinct. You've either got it or you haven't.

I guess I've got it. I've always had it. When I was a kid I was alert to any stray ball in the box. When I'm upfront for United now, I'm always on my toes. I'm alive to every chance. I'm always trying to guess where the ball is going in the next split second so I can be ready for it. I'm looking, anticipating, gambling on free balls and defensive mistakes, but this is natural ability. Guessing where to move (and then scoring when I'm one-on-one with the goalie) is a knack that some players have, some don't. And that instinct can be the difference between scoring five goals a season and scoring 25, at any level.

Whenever I play for United, I have to react differently to whatever's happening around me. If I see one of our wingers – Ronaldo or Giggsy, say – shooting from one side of the area, a gut feeling tells me to leg it to the back post. I know that the ball could get dragged wide and I might have a tap-in. If I see Scholesy or Alan Smith shooting, I always follow the ball in for the rebound. It might come my way, it might not. Even if it only falls my way once every 20 efforts, that could be enough to grab two or three extra goals a season.

It's not just about guessing the flight of a shot or pass either, it's about reading body shape. Before a ball is played from the wings or in midfield, I look to see what type of position my teammate is in as he passes. From his movement, I can roughly judge where he's looking to pass the ball, then I'll run to that space.

If I'm lucky, if I've judged everything right, I'll be running in on goal. That's when I have to be ready for the next bit: my control, my movement, and my shot. That's where training comes in.

By working on my technique constantly, I've developed muscle memory. I know instinctively what to do when a pass comes my way. If a ball comes to my chest on the penalty spot, I know without thinking how to bring it down, set myself and shoot, because I've trained my mind. I'm not the only one. All the best goalscorers in the world do it, too.

I practise it all: long shots, volleys, half-volleys, free-kicks. My movement in the box has already improved dramatically over the years through experience, plus I'm really helped by some great crossing from my teammates, like Giggsy and Ronaldo – but only when he releases the ball as quickly as he can. Don't get me wrong, Ronnie is turning into a great footballer, but when we play together, I never really know what he's going to do next.

He picks up the ball wide. I make a run.

He cuts inside. I check, make another run.

He chops back. I check again, get into an onside position.

He drills a shot in and I stand there, frustrated. It can get a bit much sometimes.

*****

We finish just after midday. At the end of each session, we warm down, relax. Some people jump into ice baths, others get into the swimming pool. Then there's the gym. It looks a bit like an old-school leisure centre: mats, weights, bikes, one of those green drapes that divides the two halves of a sports hall. Ryan Giggs sometimes does yoga in here after training. I tried it once or twice but it's not really my thing, it's too boring. For 45 minutes an instructor got me to stretch and hold my positions. When I ask Giggsy about why he does it, especially when it's so boring, he tells me that it's strengthened his muscles.

'I reckon it prolongs a player's career by increasing their flexibility,' he says.

Maybe in a couple of years I might get into it more. Right now, I don't feel like I need it.

Sometimes in training I'll work out in the gym, but only if I'm injured and can't play in the practice games or run properly. If we have a free week – that's a game on Saturday and then the following Saturday with no fixtures in-between – we'll go in as a team to work on the weights. Some players have set programmes, others do their own thing. I'll go in there occasionally, but really, if there isn't a ball around, I'm not that interested.

I just want to play football.

*****

Team spirit isn't the same as friendship. Players don't have to be great mates to be great teammates. I speak to a few lads outside of training like Rio; I play a bit of golf with some of the boys, but we don't do any more than that. They're my teammates, I see them enough during the day. It's like any profession; I have pals at work just like everyone else, it doesn't mean I have to knock about with them all the time.

That's not to say it isn't fun, though. I love going to work. The dressing room can be a right giggle. Someone's always messing around, everyone's laughing, and I buzz off stitching up some of the other lads, often with the help of Darren Fletcher. Fletch is always up for a laugh.

Today it's the turn of Quinton Fortune, our South African midfielder, to get it. We superglue his brand-new trainers to the dressing-room floor because Rio has got us going this morning. He's always stirring the lads up, willing us to play practical jokes on one another. More often than not it works. Once we've finished with Quinton he tells me that Wes Brown has been moaning.

'You should watch out because he wants to get you back for some of the pranks you've played on him,' he says.

I fall for it.

'Fletch, we should get Wes first, before he can get us,' I say.

I notice that Wes has also come into Carrington today with a flashy pair of trainers. As he showers, Fletch and I carve them apart with a knife borrowed from the team canteen, carefully arranging the sliced leather together and leaving the shoes by his locker so he won't notice the damage as he gets dried.

He pulls on his clothes and can't work out why the team are rolling about laughing. When he picks up the trainers they fall apart at the heel and the dressing room cracks up. Rio's laughing harder than everyone else because he's kick-started the whole thing.

Not everyone's happy with the joking around. Wes is moaning about his slashed trainers; Quinton's trying to pull his shoes off the floor. Some of the fitness coaches start complaining that we're not professional enough in the dressing room. Then one of the kit men complains that we're always on our phones, he says they should be banned.

'But I see you in your office on the phone,' I say. 'What's the difference?'

He shuffles around, picking up the dirty training kit. He carries on moaning about the mess. Though this time he does it under his breath.

*****

Gary Neville, Giggsy, Scholesy, all of the United players have the same routine as me at work.

In at 9.30.

Warm up.

Train.

Warm down.

After lunch, work is done for the day, but not for everyone. At half-twelve I'll walk down the corridor, past the laundry room, through reception and its fancy model of Old Trafford. I drive away from the club car-park gates where more autograph hunters are hanging around.

In the rearview mirror, I can still see The Manager's Audi.

CHAPTER

PRESSURE

FINAL PREMIER LEAGUE TABLE, 15 MAY 2005

	PLAYED	GD	POINTS
1/ CHELSEA	38	57	95
2/ ARSENAL	38	51	83
3/ UNITED	38	32	77

We're just not good enough to win the title; we can't seem to settle the team and push ahead of Arsenal and José Mourinho's Chelsea, who go on to win the league. Eighteen points separate them from us.

I'm gutted. I know the club had bought in myself and Ronnie for the long haul and that The Manager is always talking about how this has been a season of transition, but it's no consolation for me. I've come here to win league titles and trophies. Coming third is not good enough.

Still, Chelsea have looked like title winners all season; they're organised and consistent. They have Didier Drogba upfront who's strong and powerful; Arjen Robben works on one wing, Damien Duff the other. Frank Lampard orchestrates play from the middle of the park. They're also tough defensively and difficult to break down because of John Terry and Ricardo Carvalho. JT is a brilliant defender, a real leader. The Portuguese lad is hard to play against too. He's quick, he reads the game well; he's tough, he tackles hard. Chelsea deserve the title.

Our only chance of silverware comes in the FA Cup final where we face Arsenal, having beaten Exeter City, Boro', Everton, Southampton and Newcastle in the earlier rounds. I'm buzzing to be playing in an FA Cup final. I used to love watching it as a kid when I'd spend all day in front of the telly, getting dead excited as the teams got on the coaches and made their journey to the ground. I'd watch the interviews with the players and the squad as they walked around the pitch in their suits before the game. It felt like a real occasion. When I used to play footy in the park with mates we'd always talk about scoring a goal at Wembley, the pressure of The Big Day and what it would be like to take a penalty and win an FA Cup final for Everton.

Now it's happening for real.

From the opening minute we batter Arsenal. Rio has a goal disallowed for offside; Lehmann makes save after save to keep them in it. Myself, Roy Keane and Ronaldo all have chances to score, but we can't put the ball away. I hit the post; Ruud has a handful of opportunities, but he can't finish them off. Somehow, Arsenal make it to extra-time.

They're fortunate to have got this far and they know it, but I reckon their good fortune might give them a bit of extra momentum. A shot of inner belief. Sometimes I can tell when a game isn't going to go my way and today seems like one of those days.

Just keep going, Wayne. Hope for a lucky break.

The lucky break never comes.

Arsenal cling on through extra-time. Then it goes to pens even though we've been hammering them for 120 minutes. They can't believe it. They still have a chance of winning the cup. I can't believe it. I know it shouldn't have gone to pens in this game, not after the way we've played.

The Manager puts me down to take one.

'You're number four, Wayne,' he says.

No problem.

I know the penalty kick is a mental battle. Me against the goalkeeper. One on one.

A lot of the time I win.

I practise penalties every day in training. In the dressing room before a match I decide where I'm going to put the ball should we win one later in the game. Before every kick-off, I know exactly how I'm going to take the pen and how hard I'm going to hit it. If ever I have to take one in a match, I just step up and put the ball there. I never change my mind because a split second of indecision or hesitation can mess the whole thing up.

Taking the kick is a lonely moment, though. When I'm plac-ing the ball down, I shut everything out – the crowd, the oppo-sition, the keeper waving his arms. I think: *I'm 12 yards from goal, if I was running through in open play this would be easy*. It boosts my confidence. I fancy myself to score every time.

I look down. I can only hear a roar of noise – their fans whistling and jeering; our fans wishing the ball in – but it's just a buzz. The crowd doesn't even register in my head. They don't bother me at all.

All I have to do is make a good connection with my laces.

I look at the ball.

I look straight at the keeper.

I look at the ref.

Once I hear the whistle, I go, head down and make as sweet a strike as I can.

Goal!

Some players feel relieved to have scored a penalty. They figure the pressure's on them, not the goalie. I'm different. I figure it's another chance for me to put one away and I enjoy them as much as a 25-yard rocket into the top corner against Newcastle.

It's different in a penalty shootout, though. Then it's sudden death. Then it's more tense. One mistake can knock United out of a tournament, or decide an FA Cup final like this one. The walk from the centre circle to the penalty spot feels like the longest in football. I can imagine it gets to some players.

Not me. I know when it comes to my kick, I'm going to put the ball down and do the business, like with any penalty.

Not everyone's the same.

Ruud scores our first kick; Lauren scores for them.

Paul Scholes misses our second. We all feel sick when it happens, but at United we put missed pens down as being an occupational hazard. It's just one of those things.

Arsenal score again, Freddie Ljungberg.

Ronaldo puts his away. Van Persie scores for Arsenal.

I know that if I miss Number Four then they'll have a great chance of winning. I'm not thinking about that though. I'm so focused on hitting the ball sweetly as I reach the penalty area that the nerves fade away.

A look at the ball.

A look at the ref.

A look at the keeper.

Whistle, head down ...

Goal!

Not that it matters. We later lose the shootout 5–4; Scholesy's miss is enough for Arsenal to take the trophy. I get Man of the Match, but I'd swap it for a winner's medal because personal accolades mean little to me. Goals in penalty shootouts mean nothing to me. I've not worked all season to be a runner-up or to come third in the league. I certainly didn't dream about collecting a loser's medal when I was a kid, playing in the park with my mates.

Football's all about winning trophies, always has been, always will be.

*****

In the week I ring a pal from Crocky, one of the lads I used to play football with in the park.

'Remember we used to talk about what it would be like to score a penalty in the FA Cup final?' I say. 'Well, it's a great feeling. Unless you lose the shootout. And then it's really horrible.'

CHAPTER

CHANGE

The opening day of the 2005/06 season begins at home: Everton, Goodison Park. Back to all the boos and the jeers that their lot can chuck at me. Like I'm bothered. I've got plenty of pre-match habits to get my head right, as most footballers have, and before this game I pray, which is something I've started to do because Coleen's mum and dad are religious, so it's become important to me, too. I have faith now.

It's funny, I'm not afraid to be a believer in God, but I do all my praying in private. I'm not going to show it to people because I don't need to. I don't want people to see me praying every time I go on to a footy pitch. I'm not one for crossing myself as I run over the white line; I'm not looking up to the sky if ever I miss a sitter. Instead, in the away dressing room at Goodison – my United kit on, my boots laced – I go off into a quiet corner and have a moment to myself.

I pray for the health of my family and my friends.

I pray that I don't get badly injured or hurt.

I don't pray for victory or a goal, I pray for my safety.

I've got other rituals, too.

Last night I collared the club's kit man because I wanted to know exactly what combination of colours I'll be wearing the next day.

'Er, it's the home shirt tomorrow, Wayne, black shorts, black socks. Why?'

Just wondered.

What I don't tell him is that I've started visualising my performances the night before a game. As I get into bed I imagine the players I'm going to be coming up against the next day and I spend 20 minutes seeing situations where I'm in front of goal. I'm planning for what I'm going to do. I've realised that if I do my thinking before a match my head will be ready when the action starts.

I think if Everton's defender, Tony Hibbert, is weak on one side, I can exploit it. Then I see the Gwladys Street End, I see Ronaldo moving quickly out wide and firing in a cross towards me. I see how I'm going to move once the ball comes my way. My first touch is perfect, I'm getting a shot off at goal. It flies past their keeper, Nigel Martyn.

1–0!

My eyes start to get heavy, I'm drifting off to sleep. Physically, I'm winding down, but mentally I'm like a golfer standing over his ball: I'm visualising shots, living perfect results in my head. The thing is, I have to visualise every-thing in the right kit, otherwise it'll throw me out of sync if we're wearing different colours when it comes to kick-off the next day.

Everything's happening in a red shirt, black shorts and black socks.

In my mind I watch a long ball from our defence landing at my feet. I'm on the edge of the Everton box. Their skip-per, Phil Neville, is coming towards me. I know he's commit-ted, putting his tackles in hard all over the park. He dives in, skidding across the grass. I shape to shoot with my right, dropping a shoulder, before chopping the ball back inside as he passes me. I bang the ball past Martyn with my left peg.

2–0!

The next day when I wake up, I know I'm fully prepared.

Red shirt, black shorts and black socks.

When a chance comes my way, I'll be ready for it.

Funny thing is, when the game starts for real the result in my head is right, only the details are different. Before the match, the boos are louder than ever before and everyone's lobbing stick at me. Then Ruud puts us one-up in the 43rd minute and everything goes dead quiet.

Only seconds after we come out after the break, Everton defender Joseph Yobo has the ball in their half. I can see he's looking to knock it back to Nigel Martyn, and as he plays the pass, I anticipate exactly where it's going to go. I'm on it in a flash.

I'm 12 yards out with only the keeper to beat.

The ball's running nicely into my path; Nigel Martyn realises he hasn't got the advantage in distance so he stands still.

He's not coming off his line; I've got buckets of space to aim at.

I make my choice.

Bottom left.

The ball hits the net and Goodison Park goes silent again. The boos that rang out every time I touched the ball in the first half have stopped. It's great.

I love the silence here as much as I love the roar of 76,000 fans at Old Trafford.

I had it in my head that I was going to get a lot of stick this afternoon and I promised myself that if I scored a goal I wouldn't celebrate, but the abuse was so bad in the first half that it's been hard for me not to get emotional and wound up.

Sod it, I'm celebrating.

I run towards the United fans, sliding on my knees, screaming my head off as the rest of the team jump on me. Right now, I'm the only happy Everton fan in the country.

*****

As the season moves from August into September, the one thing I notice after a full year at United is that everyone tries so much harder against us, especially at Old Trafford. I expected it when I first signed – even The Manager and players like Gary Neville warned me that teams often up their game against us, but it takes a bit of getting used to. Players I competed against in a blue shirt a couple of years back seem so much more fired up when I compete against them in red, it's mad. Like Blackburn, who come to our place in September and win 2–1. They shouldn't be beating us, we're a team of top players, but we give away a couple of silly goals.

I suppose some of it is down to inexperience; we're a bit naive. Everyone knows we're a team in transition. Sure, we've got seasoned players like Giggsy, Scholesy and Gary Neville in the team; Edwin van der Sar has joined us from Fulham and he's a top goalie. But there's plenty of inexperience as well. Players like myself, Ronaldo and Darren Fletcher are still learning about breaking down teams who are desperate to defend. We don't yet know how to see out games, we haven't got much patience and it's costing us silly points.

I do everything I can to make it easier for myself. I always watch our next opponents on the telly in the week before a match, just to get a feel for what I'm coming up against. One Saturday night in October I have a Chinese takeaway with a glass of wine; *Match of the Day* is on the telly and I take a look at next week's team, Boro'. They're terrible; they lose 2–1 to West Ham.

We should beat these 10–0 next week.

When we kick off seven days later at the Riverside Stadium in the cold and the wet, they're like a different side – faster, stronger, hungrier than they were the previous week. They've been transformed. It's like the thought of playing us has turned them into a better team. It does my head in. We can't get a grip on the game. In the opening minutes, their defenders target me and Ronnie and I can't influence the play at all. Suddenly their midfielder, Gaizka Mendieta, hits a hopeful long-range shot which Edwin should save, but instead it hits the back of the net and the whole place goes mental. Boro' are so pumped up that they then score another three and we get properly thumped.

The Manager is furious afterwards.

'That was not a Manchester United performance,' he screams as all of us sit in the dressing room afterwards, staring at our shoes. 'You're not fit to wear the shirts.'

He's right and we know it. It takes half an hour before anyone can muster the energy to get into the shower.

It's not been much better in the Champions League, either. Our lack of experience and impatience means we can't break down the likes of Benfica, Villarreal and Lille in the group stages. Against Villarreal I lose my temper and sarcastically applaud the ref (Kim Milton Nielsen, the bloke who sent off David Beckham for England in the 1998 World Cup game against Argentina) when he books me for a late tackle. He then shows me another yellow and sends me off. We only win one game in the group and lose three, but it's weird because going into the last match of the group against Benfica we know that if we win, we'll qualify. Instead we lose and finish bottom of the table. Serves us right for not knowing how to break teams down when they sit back against us.

I've been on the other side of it, though. Whenever I played for Everton against United it always felt like a

My debut against Spurs at Goodison Park in August 2002. I'm wearing Gazza's number 18 shirt.

Chatting to Thierry Henry after my first League goal for Everton in the 2-1 win over Arsenal in October 2002.

Playing against the old enemy for the first time. I battered my hip in the match but there was no way I was limping off the field in a Merseyside derby at Anfield.

With my hero, Duncan Ferguson. I loved him as a kid because he was a battler. He always put a shift in.

My first ever red card against Birmingham City in 2002. I felt sick afterwards.

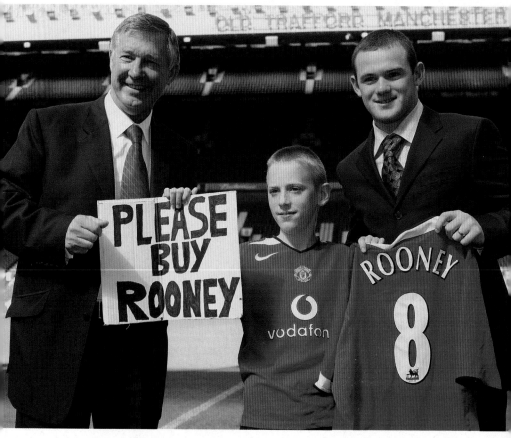

Joining Manchester United in 2004, alongside The Manager and Joe Ruane, a fan who made a sign telling the club to buy me.

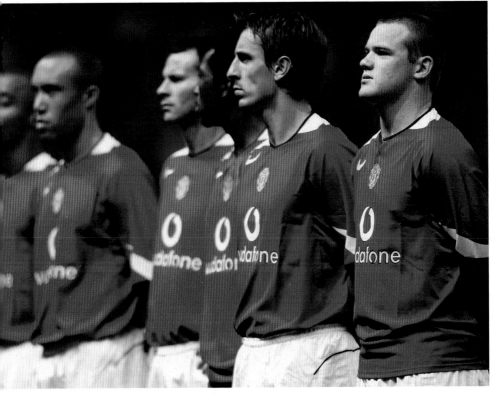

Focus. Staring at the stands before my debut against Fenerbahce in the Champions League in 2004 and thinking: *Bloody hell, this is Old Trafford.*

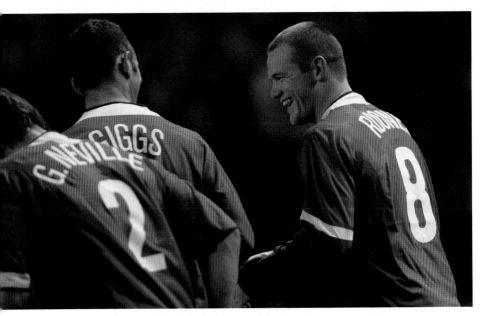

Celebrating my hat-trick against Fenerbahce. I had bucketloads of confidence in that game, it was mad.

Getting sent off in the Champions League against Villareal in 2005. It was my own fault really. I sarcastically applauded the ref when he booked me. Another lesson learnt.

Messing about with The Manager at the Stade de France, November 2005.

Captaining United against Roma in December 2007. An honour.

Meeting the fans on a United tour of Asia. It's mad when we go there – the crowds are all over us. Every time we go out camera phones point at us from every angle.

Training with Scholesy, Giggsy and Gary Nev. Those lads have been the heartbeat of United for a generation.

Winning the Champions League in 2008.

Premier League winner.

Danger men: training with Ronaldo and Nani at Carrington.
Those two have helped me to a lot of goals.

The energy of playing top flight
football summed up: the red mist
comes down whenever we lose, like
in this 2-0 defeat against Fulham in
March 2009 when I was sent off.

The buzz of scoring is like nothing else.
When it happens – like in this Carling Cup
semi final against City in January 2010,
where I scored the winning goal – I lose my
head. For five or six seconds afterwards
I honestly don't know what I'm doing.

massive game and we were always determined to defend. At Goodison, the fans were louder and players pushed the ball around at a higher tempo. When we went to Old Trafford, we battled like it was a fight to save the club. In October 2002 we even kept a clean sheet, well, for most of the game.

I was a sub that day. It was funny because when I came off the bench with 15 minutes to go, the game at 0–0, the United fans gave me loads of stick. They had their reasons, I suppose – I was a Scouser and lots had been written about me in the press. There was plenty of hype flying around about the sort of footballer I could become and it probably didn't help that I was an aggressive lad on the pitch and I loved a tackle. The boos started straightaway, but I knew that was because we were clinging on to a draw and they didn't want me to nick a winner.

Then, on 86 minutes, United scored the first of three goals.

Three!

Once they got the opener, there was absolutely nothing we could do to stop the battering. Our legs became heavier, our touch went out of the window. We were wrecked. The first goal blew us apart, like a pin bursting a balloon.

An equaliser against this lot at Old Trafford? No chance, pal.

Their second and third goals went in shortly afterwards. We were done in.

It's funny, some of the lads at United don't see the difference in our opponents – how they up their game when they play us – but I do because I love studying the game and the teams we're playing against in the league. I treat it as being part of the job. It's homework, *overtime*.

I watch Spanish and Italian football. I'll even watch the Championship teams. I don't get anything from the games lower down the leagues, but if there's a match on, I'll take a look at it because I love it. I want to know who's playing and how they're playing. Most of all, I love watching strikers. I can learn something by watching anybody, no matter what standard they're playing at.

*****

Roy Keane leaves the club in November 2005, which is massive news. The United fans love him, but he busts his foot against Liverpool in September and doesn't really play again. I guess The Manager has decided it's the end of the line for him and so Roy's off to Celtic. It hasn't helped that he's criticised some of the younger players after the battering Boro' gave us. Still, when he leaves Old Trafford it's a bit of a shock for everyone.

'It's something we'll have to deal with,' says The Manager when he gets the squad together to break the news. No big fuss is made among the players, and Gary Nev is made skipper, which seems like a sound choice to me. Gary's perfect for the job, a player's player. I know he'll do everything that's best for the team because he's a real leader and he's great for everyone around the club, not just the lads in the first team, but the reserve and youth team players, too. Whenever any of the kids have problems or questions about their contracts, they always go to him for advice.

Because of players like Gary, I've settled at United really easily. Old Trafford feels like home and being relaxed gives me self-belief – I know I can score goals and create chances for other players. A lot of the game is about confidence. With it, I'm unstoppable. Without it, I'm not the same footballer. There are some days when the goal looks huge and I just know I'm going to score. Then there are times when it seems to shrink to the size of a letterbox. All of it's in my head.

For a month in 2005/06 between the end of October and the end of November, I go a handful of games without scoring, but I keep calm, which is hard. Sometimes in the middle of a bad run of form, or a few weeks without a goal, it's easy to get wound up.

Why haven't I scored?

What am I doing wrong?

What should I be doing?

But I have to stay focused, otherwise it'll affect the way I think on the park. I shut it out. Instead, I keep going. I keep working. I know if I keep the game simple, then the goals will come. Luckily for me, when I'm not scoring for United, other players step in and do it for me, like Ruud, Ronaldo and Louis Saha, who we signed from Fulham in 2004. Louis and I really click on the pitch sometimes. He's got a lot of pace to his game and he's so good on the ball that I'm not sure whether he's left- or right-footed, even after months of training and playing with him.

The Manager knows the goals will come back too, he knows how to keep me going during a lean spell. He tells me that when I'm not scoring goals it's important that I make up for it in other areas, so in games I always chase down defenders and set up chances. I run my marker hard, pulling him wide, knackering him out. I make spaces for other players to leg it into. After the 90 minutes are done, I don't beat myself up if I haven't got a goal, but that's not the case with the other forwards at the club. When Ruud or Ronnie haven't scored in a game, they get a cob on, even if we've won. With me, if United have won I'm happy whether I've scored or not. Maybe I need more of that focus, that greed. Maybe I should be more moody if I haven't scored a goal. At the moment, though, I only get upset if we lose.

It takes four league games, but my next goal comes in a 2–1 away win at West Ham in November and then I hit a bit of a hot streak, scoring against Pompey (3–0 win), Wigan (4–0), Villa (2–0) and Birmingham (2–2). On New Year's Eve we hammer Bolton 4–1 and the team sits in second place. We're miles away from Chelsea, but I reckon we've got it in us to win the league, provided we can cut out the silly mistakes and Chelsea slip up.

PREMIER LEAGUE TABLE, 31 DECEMBER 2005

	PLAYED	GD	POINTS
1/ CHELSEA	20	34	55
2/ UNITED	20	23	44
3/ LIVERPOOL	18	17	40

We all know it's a long shot. But at United, we never give up.

*****

Ruud isn't happy. I think he knows his time at United is coming to an end and that the style of football we're playing isn't suited to him. He's still an amazing goalscorer, but the players that The Manager has brought in like Ronaldo, Louis and myself are more geared to playing quick, counter-attacking football. We play with pace; Ruud likes to slow the ball down and bring other players into the action, but we're not playing that way anymore.

I've had the feeling that he's been unhappy from the minute I signed for United. Ronnie and I have been getting the headlines and I don't think he's been too chuffed about that – it hasn't been our fault, we haven't written them, but we're definitely getting most of the attention. It's not so bad for me, I get on with Ruud, but I don't think him and Ronnie are the best of pals. There's been one or two arguments on the training ground and Ruud's become dead annoyed when Ronnie hasn't released the ball to him as quickly as he'd like.

Then The Manager drops Ruud for the Carling Cup final against Wigan in February and he's really not happy. He sits on the bench alongside our new January signings, Patrice Evra, a French full-back we've bought from Monaco, and our Serbian centre-half, Nemanja Vidic. Patrice already loves it here. He came from the sun and the sea in Monte Carlo and he knew Prince Albert of Monaco. But when it rains on the training ground, he starts dancing.

'Welcome to England!' he shouts.

It's taken Patrice and Vida a while to settle because they can't hack the pace of English football, they're shocked by it. After their first training session at Carrington they both looked absolutely wrecked. Three weeks later they still look wrecked.

I wind them both up for a laugh.

'Here, Rio,' I say in the dressing room one day, knowing they can both hear. 'These two are terrible, they can't hack it.'

Vida and Patrice chuck some abuse back, but I can tell the Premier League has been a massive shock for them both. It is for all the foreign players when they first come here.

Despite Ruud's bad mood before kick-off, we're really fired up for the Carling Cup final, having beaten Barnet, West Brom, Birmingham and Blackburn to get here. The biggest motivator, though, is the pain of losing the FA Cup final to Arsenal the previous season. It still hurts and The Manager knows it's driving us on. Before the game he's calm. We're strong favourites today, and he reckons that if we play our normal game against Wigan, we'll win.

He's not wrong. We score four, I get two. My first falls to me after the ball gets played up to Louis. He wins the header, the ball drops down and two defenders collide as they try to deal with it. The blunder leaves me with a one-on-one with the keeper and I lift the ball over his head into the corner of the net. Then I slot in my second after Rio wins a knockdown from a free-kick.

Wigan don't have anything to hit us back with, they haven't got a chance. Despite their lack of Premier League experience, both Patrice and Vida get on the pitch at the Millennium Stadium. Ruud doesn't and he's not happy. To be fair, I'd be moody in his situation, too. I know right then that he'll probably leave the club in the summer.

*****

The Carling Cup is my first United trophy but it's not enough because The Big One, the Premier League, looks like slipping away again.

Chelsea.

It's the same story as last year: they're strong up front, they defend hard all season. We run them close, though, cutting back the 11-point gap from New Year's Eve and by the end of the campaign we have a slim chance to nick the title off them if we can beat them at their place on 26 April. The snag is that they then have to lose their final games against Blackburn and Newcastle. Meanwhile, we'll have to beat Boro' and Charlton in our remaining fixtures (and score a lot of goals). If Chelsea draw with us, though, they'll win the title with matches to spare. The game is like another cup final; everything's on a knife edge.

It's a disaster for us from start to finish. Their defender, William Gallas, scores early on. Not long afterwards I go into a 50–50 tackle with John Terry, but I'm that fired up I get the ball but go straight through him. He lies still on the floor for ages and a stretcher is brought on for him but he manages to get himself together. He plays on afterwards, but he's clearly in pain. At the next corner, as we jostle in the penalty area, he whispers in my ear.

'I've got a hole in my foot where your stud landed.'

I feel bad for him, but not that bad. It's one of those things.

Get on with the game.

Then after 20 minutes, I go clean through on goal. Their keeper Petr Cech looms up in front of me and I put the ball wide. I know it's a chance to put the squeeze on Chelsea, but I've blown it. *I feel sick.*

It doesn't get any better in the second half. In fact, it's a horror show: Joe Cole scores a second for Chelsea as he wriggles past a couple of defenders and bangs a shot past Edwin; I bust my foot when I go into a challenge with Chelsea defender Paulo Ferreira. It's a nothing tackle really, but it's enough to fracture a metatarsal and it's bloody agony, though the pain is probably more mental than physical because as I leave the pitch, loads of questions race around my head.

Is the title race over?

Am I out for the World Cup in Germany in the summer?

The first is answered pretty shortly after I'm carried off. Chelsea score a third and our chances of winning the league are gone.

After the game, both me and John Terry are on crutches in the tunnel at Stamford Bridge. I reckon he's in less pain than me because he's got another Premier League winners' medal around his neck and when we bump into one another, we're both going in different directions: me to the team bus back to Manchester, him to the pitch to celebrate with the Chelsea fans. He asks for a signed shirt.

Sure, JT, here you go, mate.

When I hand it back, he sees that I've written a personal message, as well as my signature:

'To JT, can I have my stud back?'

He doesn't look too happy, but then neither do I most probably. It's my second season at Old Trafford and Chelsea have won the league both times. We've not even got close to challenging them. I look at the Premier League standings a couple of days later:

PREMIER LEAGUE TABLE, 29 APRIL 2006

	PLAYED	GD	POINTS
1/ CHELSEA	36	52	91
2/ UNITED	36	34	79
3/ LIVERPOOL	37	30	79

I'll admit it: as we make the journey back home, a little bit of doubt creeps in.

Are we going to be good enough to win the league?

CHAPTER

CHAMPIONS

Old Trafford, 20 August 2006; the first day of the season. There's a mirror by Ronaldo's seat in the Old Trafford dressing room. In the time I've been playing with Ronnie the one thing I've noticed about him is that he can't walk past his reflection without admiring it, even if we're about to play a game of football. Every match, before the team goes out for the warm-up, he runs through the same routine. The kit goes on, the boots go on. Not long after, Ronnie turns to his reflection and stares, psyching himself up for the game.

If there's one person with a bigger self-belief than Ronaldo then I haven't met him yet. He's not shy; he loves his clothes and the clobber he wears is always super-expensive and covered in shiny logos – Dolce & Gabbana, Armani, you name it, he's swaggered into the training ground wearing it, looking immaculate from head to foot. He must spend a fortune on his wardrobe.

But Ronaldo's biggest love is football.

At the training ground he tells us he wants to be The Best Player In The World, that he's desperate to be The Greatest. He has the determination about him to make it happen, too. Fair play to him, I like that attitude, but it's not for me. I'm more into helping the team to win things rather than getting any personal accolades or special gongs for the mantelpiece at home, but if Ronnie wants to be the best footy player on the planet and it helps United to our first Premier League title since I've been here, well, I'm all for it.

Ronnie's ambition isn't just talk, either. In the changing rooms at Carrington before the 2006/07 season I notice something different about him. He's bigger. He's come back from the World Cup in Germany muscly and buffed up, like he's been on the weights all summer. On the pitch in pre-season, he's started cutting out all the fancy tricks and flicks and finding an end product to his mazy runs down the park. Gary Nev is done in. During the week he has to mark Ronaldo in training matches. When he's not marking Ronnie, he's trying to do a job on Ryan Giggs. Every morning he grumbles about having to retire early, though at least he hasn't got to worry about marking Ruud in training as well. Real Madrid signed him in the summer.

I know one thing: this change in Ronaldo hasn't come about by luck. He works bloody hard all week. Some players go home straight after training, but he's usually out there with a bag of balls long after clocking-off time, working on different drills – free-kicks, headers, long-range shooting. I think it's something a lot of people haven't recognised in him just yet; fans think players like Ronaldo are born with a talent and that's it. 'Everything comes easy for him,' they say; they think he can't be coached. Part of that might be true but a lot of hard work goes into maintaining his ability. When I watch him train or see him scoring great goals for fun in pre-season friendlies, I think he really could become the best player in the world.

Now, before the first game of the season at Old Trafford, he goes through his usual pre-match routine. He looks pristine.

The lads start laughing, pulling his leg. Then he goes out and scores a cracking goal as we spank Fulham 5–1. I score two. It's United's biggest opening day win since before World War II. And we don't let up all season.

*****

The mad thing is, Ronaldo and I aren't supposed to be getting on. The papers decide we're not going to work together because of an incident that happened during the World Cup. In England's quarter-final against Portugal – *Ronaldo's Portugal* – I got tangled up with their defender, Ricardo Carvalho, and accidentally stuck a boot on him. It looked bad but actually it was a total accident. As I protested my innocence, Ronnie started waving an imaginary card around, getting in the ref's face. The official pulled out the red and I was off.

101

An early bath.

Tournament over.

When I walked to the tunnel, I knew I couldn't really blame Ronaldo for what had happened because he was trying to win the game for his country. Besides, in the first half I'd tried to get him booked for diving, so I was as bad as him really. But moments after my card, Ronaldo started winking at the sidelines, and to people watching the game on the telly it looked bad, like he was dead pleased about it. Down to 10 men, England then went out on pens and all hell broke loose – everyone immediately decided that Ronaldo and I were the best of enemies and his wink would spell trouble for United in the coming months. I knew what was in store so when I bumped into him in the tunnel after the game I gave him a heads up.

'The fans will be going mad over this one,' I said. 'They'll be trying to make a big deal of it, so we'll just have to get on with things as normal because there will be talk all summer.'

He understood, he's a bright lad, but not long afterwards the papers reckoned he was off to Real Madrid; apparently me and him weren't talking, which was absolute rubbish. The truth is, I like Ronaldo, always have done. He's a good lad, he's great to have around the dressing room. The Manager knew we'd be fine together, too. He didn't sit us down for a pep talk when we arrived for the first day back at pre-season. There was no need. He understood it would be business as usual with the two of us.

The United lads loved the drama though. Everyone gave us stick in the dressing room, and when we turned up for the first session back at the club someone even brought in a pair of boxing gloves, as if the pair of us were going to have a scrap before we warmed up for the morning. But after our first practice game together everything was as right as rain: Ronnie looked sharp and we were playing well together, everyone was. I could tell that we were going to have a cracking season.

*****

After the Fulham game, the first of 2006/07, I'm probably the most confident I've ever been in a football team because on paper United seem strong enough to tear any side apart. It's clear that with Ruud gone, The Manager wants us work on a style of football that will blow everyone away. He sets up the team to have bags of pace with myself, Ronaldo and Louis Saha upfront. We're being told to counter-attack at speed; he reckons teams will find it impossible to play against us in the coming months.

Across the park, everyone's starting to click. Darren Fletcher is maturing in midfield; Michael Carrick – Geordie lad, soft feet – joins us from Spurs in the summer and finds his rhythm pretty quickly. In pre-season friendlies, he sits in front of the back four and controls the tempo of the game, giving us extra protection in defence when everyone bombs forward. Elsewhere, Patrice Evra and Nemanja Vidic suddenly look the business. Patrice caught his breath by the end of the 2005/06 season and now he seems up to speed with the pace of English football, which is a million times quicker than anything he's had to deal with in France; Vida and Rio are shaping up to be the best centre-half pairing in world football at this moment.

After pre-season is done, we look solid. I know we can score goals for fun, I know we have the strength to sweep teams aside.

I'm right, too: the 5–1 win against Fulham is just the start.

Charlton Athletic, 3–0.

Spurs, 1–0.

Newcastle, 2–0.

Liverpool, 2–0.

Bolton, 4–0.

Everton, 3–0.

Villa, 3–0.

Watford, 4–0.

From the first day we sit at the top of the Premier League for the whole campaign (bar one or two weekends) and never look like shifting.

Spurs, 4–0.

Bolton (again), 4–1.

Blackburn, 4–1.

We've gathered enough experience to grind out ugly victories, too.

Sheffield United, 2–1.

Boro', 2–1.

Reading, 3–2.

I know we're tough enough to win games when we're not playing well. It's a sure sign that United are a title-winning team in the making.

*****

I get the Number 10. After Ruud leaves the club in the summer for Real Madrid, I go into The Manager's office. I ask him for his shirt.

'I've always loved the Number 10,' I say. 'I've always loved players like Maradona, Pele, Zidane – all the greats have been Number 10s. It's a big thing in South America, too ...'

'It's yours,' he tells me.

It's feels brilliant to play in it for the first time.

*****

There's nothing worse than getting The Hairdryer.

When it happens, The Manager stands in the middle of the room and loses it at me. He gets right up in my face and shouts. It feels like I've put my head in front of a BaByliss Turbo Power 2000. It's horrible. I don't like getting shouted at by anyone. It's hard for me to take, so sometimes I shout back. I tell him he's wrong and I'm right. Once I've cooled down, I usually realise that it's the other way round.

Mark Hughes came up with the nickname when he was here and it's stuck. The Manager knows all about it: he even told the papers that if someone challenges him in the dressing room, he has to go for them. He believes you can't avoid the confrontation, no matter who the player is. It's his way of ruling the team. Apparently he once went for keeper Peter Schmeichel, and he's six-foot four.

Often it's worse to watch another player get The Hairdryer, especially if I know they can't take it. It spurs some of the lads on, but it crushes others. I've seen The Manager shout and scream at people and when they've gone back on the pitch their heads have dropped. They've lost it. Most of the time, The Manager knows which players can take it and which players can't.

After an away game in the Champions League in 2006 against Celtic, Louis Saha misses a last-minute penalty. I play poorly. We lose 1–0. In the dressing room, The Manager lets loose. It's the worst Hairdryer I've seen. He's in Louis's face, shouting and screaming. But Louis isn't the only one getting an earful. The Manager knows I've been negotiating a new deal with the club and he saves some for me after the Celtic game.

'Players wanting more money from the club and new deals, you don't deserve anything after that performance!'

He doesn't look my way, but I know where he's aiming the comments. I don't like it, but he's right. After that performance I don't deserve an improved contract.

*****

We play away to Fulham at the end of February, and Liverpool at the beginning of March, and I know we've got it in us to be Premier League winners because along with the skill, speed and the experience, we discover a mad determination that pushes us on to score, whatever the odds. It comes from The Manager. *He's drilled that desire into every one of us over the last couple of seasons.*

'Be patient,' he says in his team meeting before the kick-off at Craven Cottage. 'You can win the game in the last five minutes today.'

Then he reminds us of our talent on the park.

'If we play the way we can – even if we don't score early on – the opposition will get tired. Chances will come our way.'

He says it again: 'Be patient.'

He's right. Even when we go a goal down thanks to Fulham's American striker, Brian McBride, and we struggle to break down the opposition (they're chasing every loose ball like their season depends on it) we keep going. I move the ball around the park quickly, tiring out the opposition. Ronnie bombs down the wing, giving his marker a horrible time. I scrap it out with Carlos Bocanegra and Philippe Christanval in the middle of their defence – I can hear them breathing hard as they try to keep pace with us. As the game wears on, gaps start to open up on the pitch and we exploit them.

A ball comes across to me and I lay it on for Giggsy to score.

Then with a couple of minutes to go, Ronaldo picks up the ball inside our own half and races at the Fulham defence. He drives the ball past their keeper and everyone goes nuts. The Manager is hugging Ronnie on the sidelines.

It's just the start though. The following week we go to Anfield and win; not that I see it because I'm off the pitch. Liverpool's skipper, Jamie Carragher, goes in on me hard. His studs rake down my shin, leaving a nasty gash. I limp out of the game, the score balanced at 0–0 and the club doctor puts eight stitches into my leg in the dressing room as the match goes on without me.

These moments are the worst. I hate being helpless, useless, away from the action. I'm anxious. I sit on the treatment table, feeling the weird stillness of an empty changing room, the muffled cheering outside. Then I hear a roar from the crowd – a big, echoing cheer. My heart sinks. I look at the club doctor, worried.

Oh no, have we gone one-down?

It doesn't really sound like a goal, though. The noise isn't big enough. I'm right. Moments later, the dressing-room door swings open with a crash and Scholesy walks in. Another red card.

He sits by his locker and lets on to me. His head drops. The game hasn't been going great for us even with 11 men, now it's a lot worse. We've defended well without offering much upfront. Without me and Scholesy, United have only a small chance of taking this game. I know a win today isn't vital to get my first ever Premier League trophy, but three points will be a massive boost.

There can only be seconds left on the clock.

The muffled cheering starts up again, then another roar, a really loud one, the kind of noise that follows a goal. I check the doctor's face; Scholesy does too, like we're waiting for his diagnosis. I can tell what he's thinking.

Oh, for 'eff's sake, Liverpool have scored the winner.

This time, my head drops. I feel ill. The pain in my leg gets a whole lot worse.

The door is kicked open again, like someone's booted it angrily, but it's our coach, Mike Phelan. A massive grin is spread across his face.

'John O'Shea's scored!'

What?

'Sheasie's scored! The final whistle's gone, we've won!'

I'm off the treatment table, the pain in my leg gone. I sprint out of the tunnel, under Liverpool's 'This is Anfield' sign and onto the pitch with Scholesy, dancing around with the rest of the lads in my dirty kit, shinpads and bloody sock.

'We're going to win the league!'

Like I need an excuse to celebrate at Anfield.

*****

Dad doesn't bother watching me when United play against Everton anymore. He still has his seat at Goodison, but when we show up in April he gives it a swerve. I don't blame him. During the last two games there, Dad has had to sit quietly while the fans around him have sworn at me and screamed all sorts, even though they've known that I'm his lad. Now he's decided he'd rather stay at home, maybe watch the highlights on the telly in the evening. I don't mind, I'd be the same if it was me watching him, but this time he misses my best game of the season – a 4–2 win that strikes a psychological blow to the title hopes of Chelsea, the one team who have been on our backs all season.

Still, it doesn't start well. We're 1–0 down at half-time, and in the dressing room word goes around that Chelsea are winning 2–1 against Bolton. The lads start chatting: it gives us the desire to have a go at the game and put some daylight between them and us in the table. In the second half, Everton score again, but we battle back with a goal from John O'Shea and a Phil Neville own goal. Not long afterwards, I put us ahead for the first time in the match. Our sub Chris Eagles scores a fourth and I clock The Manager waving his arms on the touchline. He's shouting.

'Chelsea have finished, 2–2!'

He's telling us to stay calm, to see the game out.

When the final whistle goes I know two things: a) we've put five points between us and Chelsea and taken a massive step towards winning the league, and b) Dad is miles away, safe from the boos and V-signs being fired my way.

*****

We beat City 1–0 at their place in May, Ronnie scoring the winning goal from the penalty spot and I can almost taste the party champagne. We're eight points clear at the top; Chelsea only have to drop points at Arsenal the following day for us to win the title, so I spend Sunday afternoon in my front room watching the game on the telly, praying for them to lose. I'm like a fan, one of the lads from the Stretford End. I take another look at the league table as it flashes up on the screen:

PREMIER LEAGUE TABLE, 6 MAY 2007

	PLAYED	GD	POINTS
1/ UNITED	36	57	88
2/ CHELSEA	35	40	80
3/ LIVERPOOL	37	30	67

I settle down with the remote controls and the match starts well, with Chelsea getting a man sent off and Arsenal scoring from a penalty just before half-time. I think about going to the bedroom to pick out my clothes for a Premier League winners' party with the lads, but I can't tear myself away from the TV screen.

I'm fidgeting on the sofa, hoping for one more Arsenal goal. *So this is how it feels to be a United supporter.* Coleen starts to iron a shirt for me in case I have to leave the house as soon as the final whistle blows. The texts are coming in on the phone, the lads are talking about where we can go if we win the title today – *today* – but I'm in bits.

Then the atmosphere gets really edgy because with 20 minutes left Chelsea equalise.

I start to pace around the front room; the texts stop.

Please, God, don't let them get a jammy three points.

I watch through my hands, sinking into the sofa.

So this is squeaky bum time.

Then, somehow, amazingly, Arsenal do us a favour and manage to cling on for a draw. We've done it.

'Coleen, I've won my first Premier League winners' medal!'

The phone starts to go mad again. It's sorted for the squad to meet up in a bar in the middle of Manchester and when I get there, the whole place is buzzing. There are fans everywhere – it feels like an old-school knees up, the players and the supporters mixing together, having a few beers, and I love it. When I stand at the bar to get some drinks, I look behind me. All I can see are dozens of fans with their arms up, their mobiles in the air filming the party.

My head's spinning and it's not the bevvies. All through the season, I've asked the older players – Giggsy, Gary Neville, Scholesy – the same question about winning a title:

How does it feel?
What's it like?
Do you feel different?

They all say the same thing: 'The first one is always the best, Wazza. You never forget it.'

All I know is that it's the greatest buzz I've ever had in football and I don't want it to end.

*****

The next day we have to be in at Carrington for a photoshoot to mark our title win. Nine a.m. I've only had a few hours of sleep, though I'm not the only one. It's a beautiful day, The Manager's all smiles for the cameras, but some of the lads look rotten, tired, like they've been out all night. Ronaldo even wears a cap.

CHAPTER

EUROPE

It's May. I'm walking down the steps of AC Milan's cavernous San Siro stadium, a route that leads the United team from our dressing room and onto the pitch. It's the second leg of the Champions League semi-final and we're one game away from the biggest match in club football.

Once I'm in the warm, spring air, 80,000 AC Milan fans scream and shout at me; they whistle and jeer. The noise seems so loud that I reckon it could snap me in half if I allowed it to weigh me down mentally. The atmosphere is heavy, pressurised. High up in the stands – in the seats that seem a million miles away – banners are being unfolded. Firecrackers and flares fill the air with smoke. The supporters in the stadium seem to hang right over the players.

Surely that lot are going to cave in on us at any minute?

I start juggling a ball on the pitch, like you do, stretching, warming up with the rest of the lads, when all of a sudden a series of explosions go off, like hundreds of old cars backfiring at the same time.

Bang! Bang! Crash!

What the hell is that?

The deafening handclaps from Queen's 'We Will Rock You' echo around the ground and a huge roar explodes from the crowd. Then I see Gennaro Gattuso, Milan's midfielder, the bloke they call 'The Growl' because he always snaps at his opponent's heels like an angry Rottweiler. He's sprinting out of the tunnel, wild-eyed, long-haired. He races across the field, past our players who are staring at him like it's the craziest thing they've ever seen. The Milan fans go berserk; the stadium is rocking. Then, one by one, Gattuso's teammates casually amble out onto the pitch to mild applause and pick up their warm-up bibs. They've probably seen this stunt a million times before, but it's enough to get me thinking: *This is mad. There's nothing quite like the Champions League.*

I've been in this situation several times now, playing massive European teams in amazing stadiums. Competing on the continent can definitely be a bit weird. Gattuso's sprint across the grass isn't the half of it, though. I remember when the team went to Roma in April. The walk from the pitch to the dressing room was so long that by the time we got there at half-time, The Manager only had a few moments to give his team talk. Then we had to walk all the way back to play again.

The most intimidating atmosphere I've ever been in was at Beşiktaş in Turkey (where we play a couple of years later). The crowd were incredible. The fans turned their backs to the pitch and started jumping up and down together. When I came off in the second half after being subbed, one of their supporters gobbed in my face and some stuff – rubbish, probably – was luzzed in my direction. It took all my mental strength not to react and punch the fella who did it. I know he wouldn't have done it to me if he was passing me in the street, but in a big crowd he figured he could get away with it. He could hide. I sat in the dugout afterwards and threw my boots to the ground. It was all I could do to get the anger out of my system.

The crowds sound different in Europe, too. In Premier League stadiums the fans sing and shout loads, which really gives the players a lift and creates an amazing atmosphere. In Spain and Italy, they whistle and jeer. In Germany, whenever a sub comes on, the announcer shouts the first name of the player and the crowd shouts his surname in a deep roar. It sounds really intimidating.

When I'm in grounds like the San Siro today or the BJK İnönü Stadium – Beşiktaş's ground in Istanbul – I'm never sure what's going to happen with the crowd. Sometimes it's great, sometimes it can be quite unsettling. In Roma's Stadio Olimpico, trouble kicked off between the fans. It didn't really affect the players, but we knew something was happening because we could see all the riot police in the stands with their shields and helmets. At times like that I just have to focus on the game and get on with my football. *Shut out the madness.*

*****

I love playing in the Champions League because it's an entirely different game to playing in the Premier League. It's a lot harder for starters and I know I have to take my chances. With all due respect, if we're playing the likes of Norwich or Southampton in the league, I can miss one or two crosses because a couple more will probably come my way later on in the game. In Europe, I know I'm only likely to get a few scoring opportunities – if I'm lucky – because the standard of football is so high. I have to make sure I take those chances when they come along.

The refs are generally good in Europe, too. They talk to the players, more than they do in the Premier League. In England, the FA ask footballers to respect the officials more, but the refs won't speak to us when we're on the pitch. They won't communicate. They need to give respect too. It's the same for the fans: the refs should come out and explain their decisions after a game; they should admit to the mistakes they've made. I know I've scored some goals myself where I've been offside, ahead of my marker, right in front of the linesman, but he hasn't flagged; United have conceded goals that were miles offside. How hard would it have been for that official to have apologised afterwards? If he goes into a post-match interview and says, 'From where I was standing he looked onside. I'm sorry, I got it wrong,'

I'd think, 'Fair enough, at least he's admitted he's made a mistake.'

The sad thing is, they never do.

Refs are like players, though, they have bad games. And any footballer can see when it's happening. They book us for diving when we've been fouled, they give silly penalty decisions. I think any fan can understand the frustrations of a player when they've been hacked down only to be booked for simulation afterwards. And the most annoying rule we have to work with is the appeal system. If I've been booked for diving, even though TV replays show it's a foul, I can't overturn the yellow card afterwards.

I understand it's a difficult job for the refs, though, and I personally wouldn't mind video evidence in the game. It works in rugby, so why not in football? When there's been an important incident in the area – a penalty decision, or the ball bouncing down off the bar and onto the goal line – everyone spends a minute or two arguing with the officials anyway. That time could be better spent looking at a TV replay. It would only take a few seconds.

The refs in the Champions League understand that the game isn't about them. They understand the players more. And I know they're the best refs in the game because I've never really noticed them when I've been playing.

*****

To get to the Champions League semi-final against Milan, we play some blinding football, including an 8–3 aggregate win over Roma in the quarter-finals. We lose the first leg 2–1 at their place and the Italians, foolishly, think that the game is won. A few of their players start giving it, making out to the press that they're going to hammer us at Old Trafford.

You lot don't know Old Trafford.

On the night we're pumped up, confident. Michael Carrick scores after 11 minutes.

Alan Smith gets one a few minutes later.

I score straight afterwards.

Ronaldo, 44 minutes.

It's a shooting gallery; Roma are shell shocked.

Not so cocky now.

At one point, just before half-time, I have to look to the scoreboard to remind myself of how far ahead we are. We've scored that many goals.

After 90 minutes we run out 7–1 winners.

Time to face Milan in the semis.

I feel confident we can turn the Italians over because a lot of teams are struggling to live with our pace and fitness. I also know now that playing Champions League football can be tactically challenging, like a game of chess, and The Manager always likes to have a game plan. This usually means he wants us to score an away goal and not concede at home, and he tells us the match against Milan will be no different. In the Premier League it's more straightforward, we go out to win every game, but that's not the case in Europe when sometimes a 1–1 draw or a 2–1 defeat on our travels is a good result because we've scored an away goal. The key is to stick to the game plan as best we can.

At Old Trafford in the first leg against Milan, the game plan goes out of the window. We score early through Ronnie, but then their Brazilian striker, Kaka, scores twice before the break. As we walk in at half-time, I know we're in trouble.

Milan have got two away goals, this is going to be an uphill slog.

The Manager doesn't seem too upset.

'There's a long way to go lads,' he says. 'Keep working.'

Playing against AC Milan is mad. I grew up watching Italian games on Channel 4 as a kid, and I loved it. Every Sunday afternoon, after playing football in the morning, I'd settle down to watch the likes of Alen Boksic, Fabrizio Ravanelli, Edgar Davids and Zinedine Zidane. It was brilliant.

Now I'm playing against Paolo Maldini and Alessandro Nesta, legends of the Italian game.

I'm buzzing.

In the second half, we push and push and push. I score in the 59th minute. Not long afterwards, at a corner, I hear heavy breathing, panting. It's Nesta and Maldini. They're battered. I can see they want the game to end – our fitness and speed is killing them. *These are knackered. We can get a winner here.*

In injury time it happens. A ball comes in from Giggsy. It's one of those rare Champions League chances so I make the most of it. I smash the pass early, 20 yards out, catching the keeper off guard. The ball pings into the back of the net.

3–2!

It's only a slim lead, but in the dressing room after the final whistle, we're confident we can take them at their place. I know if we score an away goal, we'll rattle them, especially if it comes in the opening stages of the game. And that might be enough to get us through to the final.

How naive am I?

Milan score early in the return and kill the tie. Then they blow us away. Kaka is unplayable; in Dutch midfielder Clarence Seedorf – all killer passes and strong tackles – they have trophy-winning experience in bundles. Gattuso defends tightly, doing a job on Ronaldo, stopping him from racing down the wing, closing him out for the entire game. *We just can't break them down.*

We get done, 3–0; 5–3 on aggregate.

Milan are a class apart.

*****

I've never known anyone to be so focused on success as The Manager, and he wants the whole squad to think like him. We've won the 2006/07 league title with a few games to spare, but when we lose our final game of the season, 1–0, at home to West Ham, he's furious. He gets us into the dressing room at full-time and lays into us, just because we've blown a meaningless match.

Hang on, we're about to be presented with the Premier League trophy. Most sides would be celebrating in the dressing room, getting ready for the champagne and the photos!

Not us. We're staring at the floor like school kids, The Manager giving us The Hairdryer.

As I sit there, my ears burning, I'm reminded of Gary Nev's advice about us never being allowed to think that 'we've made it'. He's right, but it doesn't make me feel any better. The Manager shouts the dressing room down. After the rollicking it takes a while before everyone cheers up enough to put their Premier League-winning smiles back on. We're too busy thinking about how important it is to win the next trophy.

*****

Our FA Cup run, 2006/07:

Third round: Manchester United 2 Aston Villa 1 (Larsson, Solskjaer)

Fourth round: Manchester United 2 Portsmouth 1 (Rooney 2)

Fifth round: Manchester United 1 Reading 1 (Carrick)

Replay: Reading 2 Manchester United 3 (Heinze, Saha, Solskjaer)

Sixth round: Boro' 2 Manchester United 2 (Rooney, Ronaldo)

Replay: Manchester United 1 Boro' 0 (Ronaldo)

Semi-final: Manchester United 4 Watford 1 (Rooney 2, Ronaldo, Richardson)

The FA Cup final between United and Chelsea is held at the new Wembley and it's a big deal. Playing in Cardiff was great, but being in a final at the new Wembley is something special – there's a real sense of occasion to it. I remember the last time I went to the old Wembley as a kid in 1995. I watched Everton beat Blackburn Rovers in the Charity Shield. Before that, I'd watched them win the FA Cup in the same year when they beat Man United, 1–0.

To be playing here is a real buzz.

The Manager is buzzing too. He has a respect for José Mourinho. The Chelsea boss is arrogant, he's got personality and confidence, he's brilliant for the league. The pair of them enjoy competing with one another in big games like this one.

There's a problem with the Wembley pitch, though. It's crap. It doesn't live up to the occasion and shortly after kick-off I can tell it's going to be a tough afternoon. Everyone seems unsteady on their feet, I can feel different forces running through the muscles in my legs and it takes extra effort to remain balanced. I'm not the only one. The turf soon takes its toll on all the players. People are slipping over, everyone's touch become nervous, unsteady.

It's a rubbish game from the kick-off and boring for the fans to watch, because neither team can build any momentum, and nobody looks like scoring. The Manager plays me upfront on my own and sets us up to counter-attack, but both sides seem more concerned with not losing the game rather than going all out to win it. We quickly cancel one another out.

The final moves into extra-time. Our best chance of nicking it comes when I slide a ball across to Giggsy who's racing into the penalty area. He's only three yards out, the goal's on a plate, but he can't quite get a full touch on the ball. Chelsea's keeper Petr Cech makes the save, but the ball looks like it's gone over the line.

Goal! It's gone in!

We all appeal, not that the ref's having any of it, and my mind flashes back to our last FA Cup final.

Arsenal.

It's funny how my brain works when I'm on a football pitch. I think I know what's coming next (*What number penalty am I going to be taking this time?*), when, all of a sudden, 116 minutes into the game, Didier Drogba scores and one half of Wembley goes mental; the other half gets deja vu. I can't believe it, it's like 2005 all over again. We've been sucker-punched.

There's only a few minutes left, so we chuck everything at them, but this is a Mourinho team and they begin using every trick in the book to run the clock down and see out the game.

They fall over.

They take ages over throw-ins.

They roll around after tackles.

Don't get me wrong, I've pulled the same tricks to see out games. It's all part of the job, but when we're on the receiving end of it, it's not nice.

I've promised myself that I'll never cry on the football pitch, whether the emotion comes from winning a

Champions League trophy or losing the league. But as the final whistle goes I'm close to breaking down. I can feel the lump in my throat. My heart is pumping, my lungs are heavy. It's bloody horrible.

Don't cry.

Hold it in.

I've learned by now that if we don't win the league, it's not because of one game or one person, it's because of the squad and all 38 matches on the fixture list. If we lose a cup final, it's all on that one game. And losing to Chelsea in the final minutes of extra-time is just about the worst I've ever felt as a footballer.

CHAPTER 10

SACRIFICE

I sit in Carlos Tevez's car.

Carlos has only been at the club five minutes – he's signed for us on loan from West Ham after they came close to relegation at the end of last season, but he virtually kept them up on his own. He's that good a player. Now he's at United for the beginning of the 2007/08 campaign and we've already hit up a pretty good understanding in pre-season training, both on and off the pitch.

Off it, we're taking it in turns to give one another lifts. On it, we're clicking, scoring goals, which I think will come as a bit of a surprise to some people because there's been a lot of talk in the papers that we won't work well together. The fans reckon we're too similar, that we play in an identical role, but judging by our work at Carrington, I don't think there's going to be a problem.

In practice games Carlos and I seem to have an understanding: I know where he's going to run; he knows where I'm going to be whenever he has the ball. Sometimes that connection just happens in football. It's like the pair of us are telepathic, like we've been playing together all our lives. It's crazy, no one can explain why it happens with strikers but when it does click, the goals come easily.

It's a good job we have that connection because Carlos doesn't speak our lingo. Even though he's been in the country a year, he hardly says a word of English, but I don't think he's a soft lad; I reckon he knows more than he's letting on. My guess is that he can't be arsed to talk in English. Still, he seems to understand me when I shout at him. Not like Basil Fawlty in *Fawlty Towers*, but when I'm yelling at him in a game, looking across at him angrily or applauding something that he's done, Carlos can see exactly what it is that I want from him.

Luckily for Carlos, there are a few lads in the dressing room who speak his language and they seem happy to translate for him. Nani and Anderson have signed for a combined £30 million from Sporting and Porto respectively, and they can have a crack with him. Nani has only been learning English for a few weeks, but he helps Carlos with the basics. Anderson has been learning from his Xbox by the looks of things. We've been playing a computer war game called SOCOM (named after the US Special Operations Command) in the hotel on the nights before our pre-season friendlies.

For the first few weeks, Anderson hadn't spoken a word of English, then in training he started shouting phrases from the game.

'He's killed me!'

'He's in the generator room!'

Anderson's also the scruffiest bloke I know. He often arrives at training in a pair of shorts, his headphones on, and wearing flip flops. Everyone's always giving him stick.

If those two aren't around to help out Carlos then Patrice often steps in because he speaks just about every language going. The club translator has been giving him lessons and now he watches DVDs in English. If any of the foreign lads can't understand what The Manager wants, they'll usually nudge Patrice. He translates as best he can.

The other morning, while The Manager was trying to get his point across to Carlos and Nani, I thought about being in a place where I wasn't able to communicate with the players around me. I couldn't imagine not being able to understand everyone in the dressing room. If I had signed for a team abroad when I left Everton a few years back rather than United, I would have wanted to know exactly what the boss was saying at half-time. I'd have wanted to know what my teammates were talking about. It would have driven me mad if I'd been sitting there as the other lads talked to one another around me. They could have been slagging me off and I wouldn't have known.

Because of Carlos and Anderson's arrival there's another addition to the dressing room: a weird Tardis-shaped pod. It looks like an upright sunbed but it won't top up a Hollywood tan because it's designed to give the South American lads a boost of vitamin D. When someone's used to playing in the sun and the heat of Argentina or Brazil all their lives, Manchester's weather can be a bit of a shock, I suppose. This machine gives them all the vitamins they don't get from the Carrington climate.

*****

We're Premier League champions but we start the campaign like mid-table strugglers.

> Manchester United 0 Reading 0
> Portsmouth 1 Manchester United 1
> Manchester City 1 Manchester United 0

I bust my foot against Reading; Ronaldo gets sent off against Portsmouth because the ref thinks he's head-butted their midfielder, Richard Hughes. We both miss the defeat against City and the club slips into 17th spot; I don't get off the treatment table for six weeks. It's a bad start and the atmosphere around the training ground is gloomy.

From the stands I watch us as we get a result against Spurs at home. And then a crazy thing happens: Ronnie takes the season by the scruff of the neck. I can't believe it, he's been looking good for a couple of seasons now, but suddenly everything he touches turns to gold, even the highlights in his hair. It's incredible to see him play. He batters defences and turns full-backs inside out; he scores goals from mad angles. His pace is frightening and he wins us points in games when we look like getting nothing. He must be giving managers and defenders nightmares.

He bangs in goals against Birmingham, Wigan, Arsenal, Blackburn Rovers, Fulham, Derby, Everton, Sunderland, West Ham, a hat-trick against Newcastle in a 6–0 spanking; more goals against Reading, Portsmouth. He scores five goals in the group stages of the Champions League and we top our group as unbeaten winners above Roma, Sporting Lisbon and Dynamo Kiev. Managers can't work out whether he's playing as an out-and-out striker or as a winger. He leaves defences in bits, but the rest of us are pulling our weight, too. I return from injury and start scoring a lot of goals. And with myself, Ronnie, Tevez, Nani and Louis Saha (who's struggling for fitness) we have the best strike force in the league, probably Europe.

As the season moves into the Christmas period, Ronnie is the difference, though. He looks good on making his promise of being the best player in the world.

I think: *Yeah, he's the sharpest around.*

In training I can tell the lads are all thinking the same thing: *Bloody hell, don't kick Ronnie too hard, we're going to need him on Saturday.*

*****

PREMIER LEAGUE TABLE, 20 APRIL 2008

	PLAYED	GD	POINTS
1/ UNITED	35	54	81
2/ CHELSEA	35	36	78
3/ ARSENAL	35	37	74

As the season comes to an end, we're nearly 20 goals better than Chelsea, which is worth a point. I'm scoring, Carlos is scoring. Ronaldo seems to get a goal in every game. He bangs in two against Newcastle (another battering, 5–1), two against Bolton (2–0), he also scores against Derby (1–0), Liverpool (3–0), Villa (4–0), Boro' (2–2) and Arsenal (a 2–1 win). He's developed this crazy technique for his free-kicks – he hits the ball off the laces of his boot and it swerves and spins and twists in the air so the keeper can't quite suss which way it's going to go. He scores from so many dead balls that I spend ages watching him practice in training, but I can't work out quite how he does it. He seems to plant his standing foot alongside the ball so hard that it pops up slightly – which means he's almost striking the ball on the volley. This technique gives him a dip in his shot, but even when I study him – kick after kick after kick – I can't pull it off when I try the same trick.

Ronaldo's form means that he's now started playing upfront, while I'm on the wing. I don't mind too much, anything for the team, but I'd rather play as a striker. On the flanks I can't express myself in a game in the way that I'd like (but I know I can be a match winner wherever I play) and I also have to work a lot harder (which I don't mind). Playing on the wings is a lot different though. Legging it up and down the pitch for 90 minutes can be knackering.

The annoying thing is, Ronaldo can play on the flanks; it's his role. But Ronnie's the best player in the world at the moment and he's a massive threat upfront. I don't moan about it. I don't go into The Manager's office with a cob on. I never walk into training and say, 'I'm not playing unless I play upfront.' I just get on with things.

Then Ronnie scores a header against Roma in the Champions League quarter-finals that's so good it could have been put away by Alan Shearer. We're playing them at their place, the Stadio Olimpico – always an intimidating ground to go to – and with the score balanced at 0–0, Scholesy hangs a cross from the right-hand side of the box to the penalty spot. It doesn't look like it's aimed at anyone in particular at first, but then Ronaldo steams into the area having legged it from the halfway line. He jumps up, all the muscles in his neck straining as he thumps the ball past their goalie, Doni. It's one of the best headers I've ever seen.

With the away goal, the whole team becomes pumped up with confidence. I stick the ball in the net when the goalie fumbles it and we win the game 2–0. Then Carlos scores for us in the 1–0 home leg victory to put us into the semis with Barça, probably the best team in the competition.

*****

The first leg takes place in the Nou Camp – a stadium I'd always dreamed of playing in. I'd been there as a lad when we went to the city on a school trip and I was blown away by the size of the ground as we walked around it in our uniforms, rucksacks over our shoulders. I couldn't believe my luck when we bumped into the Barça goalie, Ruud Hesp, outside and we all got autographs. I thought: *How unbelievable must it be to play footy in here?*

When I get inside for the first time with United I discover the enormity of the Nou Camp.

This place is unreal.

I can't believe how high the stadium is, how big everything seems. The club have built a chapel in the tunnel for their players to pray in. When we get onto the grass for the first time, I see they've positioned speakers all around the pitch. Each one plays the noises from the crowd, so it's extra loud for the teams when they're on the pitch. It's like being at a rock gig, the sound is so huge.

We're not intimidated though, because we have another game plan. All week we've been working on how to break Barça down with our assistant coach, The Manager's right-hand man, Carlos Queiroz. One afternoon at training, he placed mats down on the floor in the club gym. They were laid out in the shape he wanted us to be in when Barça had the ball. When he positioned Scholesy's mat side by side with Michael Carrick's in the central midfield position, I noticed there was nothing between them.

'That's the distance I want you to be together on the pitch,' he said. 'Don't move too far apart, otherwise their midfielders will pick you off.'

The lads started looking at one another like he was mad, but we knew we could trust him. Tactically he's been brilliant for us. He knows exactly how we should play and he always sets up the team to win games. He has experience, having worked with Real Madrid and South Africa; The Manager knows Carlos gives us an edge when we're planning a game because he understands how to tactically win matches, especially when we're playing away from home, like against Barça.

When the team is announced, The Manager tells me he's playing me on the right flank again; England midfielder Owen Hargreaves is right-back. Ronaldo is upfront with Tevez behind him. It's hard to take at first, but when the game starts I work all over the pitch, tracking back, running the wing, putting tackles in all over the park. The aim is to defend hard and hit them on the break. It nearly pays off in the third minute when one of their defenders handles the ball at a corner.

Penalty!

The ref gives it, but when Ronnie steps up he smacks the ball against the post. I know we've blown a great opportunity to get an away goal.

When the team misses a chance like that it takes the wind out of our sails for a brief moment – an away goal against a brilliant side like Barça would be invaluable. The miss is forgotten pretty quickly though. We dig in deep and I barely get forward. I hardly make it to the box. I'm that focused on not letting Barça score that I only put in one cross all game. Instead of creating chances I track their left-back Eric Abidal, who loves to get forward. Every time he pushes on I stay with him, trailing his runs, cutting out passes. Their central midfielder, Andrés Iniesta – a maestro, always making the game tick with his quick passing – keeps cutting inside from the Barça left, making it even harder.

Bloody hell, I'm working, working, working. This is doing me in.

I'm also playing through the pain. During the recent game against Blackburn Rovers I was smashed by their centre-half, Ryan Nelsen, in a tackle. The game finished up a 1–1 draw, but the personal damage was severe. Nelsen's knee caught me in the hip and it's badly bruised. Before the game, the doc put a pain-killing injection in my backside which was probably more painful than the sensation in my hip. Now, as the injection wears off, I'm in agony.

The game is on a knife edge; we're holding Barça, they're dominating possession. Scholesy and Michael Carrick are staying tight in the middle; Carlos's trick with the gym mats is paying off. It's probably our best defensive performance of the season so far and we scrape a goalless draw. I know it's not the most attacking performance by us, and afterwards I realise that playing out wide is not a position I love, but as long as I'm on the pitch and United are one step closer to getting into a cup final, then I'm made up.

*****

We play Chelsea away and Barça at home in the same week. If we beat Chelsea at Stamford Bridge on the Saturday we'll need one more point from our final two games to win the Premier League. If we get a result against Barça at Old Trafford, we'll be in the Champions League final in Moscow. It's a mad period in the season and it's not being helped by the fact that my hip still isn't right. I'm in a lot of pain. I'm not the only one. When the Chelsea match gets under way, Nemanja Vidic gets a knee in the face during the first half and has to go off. Chelsea score just before half-time. Then, in the 57th minute I latch onto a poor back pass from Ricardo Carvalho and draw the game level. Almost as soon as the ball hits the back of the net, my hip gives out. Pain shoots up and down my leg and I can barely celebrate. It's agony. The Manager takes me off straightaway and the scans afterwards tell me one thing: *You won't be playing in the second leg against Barça, Wayne.* I'm gutted. United eventually lose 2–1 against Chelsea, meaning we'll need to win our next two league matches to retain the title. I'm on the sidelines and unable to help the team out.

A couple of days later I go to Old Trafford for the second leg of the semi-final like every other fan and watch through my hands as Barça try to pick us apart. Scholesy scores a great goal, a 25 yarder, to put us in the driving seat, but shortly afterwards the match turns into a one-sided affair: Barça in attack, United in defence. It's horrible to see. Every time they get the ball, I'm convinced they're going to score.

Their striker Lionel Messi has a chance.

Iniesta has a chance.

Thierry Henry has a header at the end of the match but he can't put it away.

Now I understand just what the fans must go through during games of this importance. My heart's in my mouth all the time, I feel nervous. Sick. Stressed. When the final whistle goes I'm suddenly struck with this mad wave of relief, and then a glowing sense of satisfaction.

We're in the Champions League final.

The biggest game in club football.

*****

We beat West Ham in our penultimate game of the season, which leaves us needing a win at Wigan on the last day of the campaign to take the title. We're tied at the top of the table with Chelsea on points, ahead on goal difference. The Wigan game is like a cup final because if we lose or draw and Chelsea win against Bolton, then they take the title. If we both draw, United win the Premier League.

Before the kick-off, the fans are up for it. We're up for it, but typically so are Wigan – I know that they want to ruin our party. As the game starts, everyone's nervous but focused on the job, and by half-time, we're a goal up, a Ronaldo penalty. As we walk off the pitch nobody can really tell how Chelsea are doing. The Manager isn't helping – he reckons he hasn't heard anything.

We know he has.

In the dressing room, as everyone sucks on their energy drinks, we hassle the coaches, the physio, Albert the kit man, anyone who might give us a clue. We're all asking the same thing.

'Are Chelsea losing?'

Each one of them shrugs, shakes their heads, makes out they haven't heard us. In the second half we get another goal, putting the game to bed and bringing the title back to Old Trafford. It doesn't matter what Chelsea do after that (they draw 1–1), the league is ours.

Afterwards I walk around the pitch, waving to friends and family again, but this time I think about playing for Everton in 2002 when I watched United win the title on our patch. Goodison Park was nearly empty. The only people in the ground were their fans at one end. I was in the tunnel watching it all, feeling sick with jealousy, thinking the same thing as everyone else in the ground not connected with United.

I need that to be me one day.

It's taken a few years but as I walk round the pitch with Scholesy and Giggsy and Ronaldo at the JJB Stadium, I get the buzz of celebrating a title win in a nearly empty football ground. I'm bouncing. It doesn't matter that there's only a few thousand United fans here, it feels like a cup final win.

Later that night we celebrate, but it's not as rowdy as our night out in Manchester last season. The players and their wives and girlfriends are attending the club player of the year awards rather than drinking in a city bar. Nobody's really up for it though. Everyone's thinking of the challenge ahead – doing a league and Champions League double. We're playing Chelsea in the final in Moscow next week after they defeated Liverpool in the other semi. Still, after a beer, I sit with Michael Carrick and the pair of us try to liven things up a little. We get on a microphone and start singing.

'Champione! Champione! Ole, ole, ole! Champione, Champione …'

We tail off. When I look around the room, no one else is singing with us. The older lads like Giggsy, Paul Scholes and Gary Neville have been here before. They know there's more hard work to come. They know we can do all the celebrating we want after Moscow. Fair play, they're right.

Their experience runs through this whole club.

CHAPTER
11
MOSCOW

Nothing prepares me for the size of a Champions League final, not even the semi-final against Barça. In the week leading up to the game, everyone's excited, everyone's talking about it. I go to training and hear stories from the lads who were there for the 1999 final when we beat Bayern Munich 2–1. Players like Gary Nev and Giggsy tell me how mad it was when we thieved the winner in injury time. I chat to some of the ex-players like Ole Gunnar Solksjaer, who scored the last-minute winning goal. He's been working with the strikers at Carrington. He tells me about the buzz of playing in the final and the noise of the fans in the ground afterwards.

In a magazine interview, Teddy Sheringham even relives the team talk at half-time. We were a goal down when, apparently, The Manager went into the dressing room and started staring at the team. He pointed to the door.

'Go out there and take a good look at that trophy,' he said. 'Because if you don't get back into the game in the next 45 minutes, that's the closest you're going to get to it.'

This week, the whole country is excited because it's an all-English final.

Manchester United v Chelsea.

The day before the game we fly to Russia, The Manager gets all the players together for a meeting and makes us study a DVD of the 1999 final. I can barely remember seeing it the first time around. I was only 13 back then. It was on at home in Crocky and I saw it on the telly with my dad and my brothers.

When I watch the game now, I can't believe how much Bayern Munich battered us.

They should have been three or four up at half-time. No way should we have won 2–1.

Then The Manager gives one of his team talks.

'That game is the history of the club,' he says, turning the sound off, the screen still playing pictures of David Beckham running round with the trophy after the final whistle. 'It proves that as a team we never give in. Bayern Munich should have been out of sight after 45 minutes, but because they weren't, we knew we'd get a chance to get back into it. When we did, we punished them with an equaliser. We still believed we were going to win the game when the clock went into injury time. And that's exactly what happened.'

He shows us the team celebrations afterwards. Teddy Sheringham, David May, Peter Schmeichel hugging one another. The Bayern players sitting on the grass looking gutted. Paul Scholes and Roy Keane in their suits, suspended for the game. They're jumping around with the lads, the Champions League trophy in their hands.

Then he tells us he wants to see the same from us afterwards in the final against Chelsea.

'There will be times in the 90 minutes when Chelsea are going to be on top,' he says. 'But you'll have to keep your focus, keep your heads. If you do that, we'll create chances and win the game.'

He turns the box off. Everyone in the room is sitting still, dead quiet.

'And remember,' he says. 'No regrets.'

*****

Moscow, 15:42.

I'm in my hotel room, several hours before we line up with Chelsea on the pitch.

I'm going mad.

Today is the longest day ever.

The kick-off for the game is at 10.45 tonight and we've got hours to kill before we even travel to the stadium. I'm desperate to leave my room and play, warm up, kick a footy around, anything. It's going to be ages before we can even get into our pre-match routine, so I try to sleep, but I can't.

I watch the telly. It's boring.

I sit. I'm fidgety.

I stand. I pace around the room, listening to tunes on my iPod.

This is a nightmare. I've been chatting to some of the Chelsea lads during the week and I know they're probably just as excited as I am. They're probably going through the same thing. I also know we've got an England game coming up next week and if we lose tonight, I'm never going to hear the end of it.

We cannot lose this game.

I'm anticipating everything about the match. The dressing room, the crowd, the walk to the pitch, my first touch of the ball. I try to switch off, to focus on scoring, but for six hours all I can think is: *How good would it be if we win tonight?*

The worst part of being a footballer, I reckon, is the waiting. Sitting on my backside, hanging around like I am now. It's amazing the amount of waiting I do as a Premier League player. I compete for 90-plus minutes on a weekend, but before that I hang around for hours doing nothing. Nothing but waiting; waiting and thinking about what might happen.

This game against Chelsea tonight, the biggest club game in the world, is just the same as any other home match really. We trained this morning, got on the team coach and started the wait. Then we came back to the hotel and waited some more. We ate, talked tactics, had a massage and waited. Every weekend is the same as today: moments of action and loads of waiting around. It can be really boring sometimes, a bit like being caged up, even in a city as far away and as mad as Moscow, because it's not like I can go for a walk outside and see the sights.

I wish I could take a pill and fall asleep. I want to wake up and for it to be time for kick-off.

The wait is the hardest part; the game tonight will make it all worthwhile. But only if we win.

*****

The hanging around is broken up by a team meeting. The Manager names his side:

1/ Edwin
3/ Patrice
4/ Owen Hargreaves
5/ Rio
6/ Wes
7/ Ronnie
15/ Vida
16/ Michael Carrick
18/ Scholesy
32/ Carlos

10/ I'm up front with Carlos, Ronnie's on the left wing.

Sound.

When the waiting ends and it's time to work, I sit at my seat in the dressing room. Red shirt, white shorts, white socks. Footy boots on. I pray.

I'm ready.

The Manager's ready, too. He walks around the dressing room in his grey club suit, white club trackie top pulled over his jacket. He gets us going again with another one of his team talks.

'Remember the history of the club,' he says. 'The game against Bayern. Think about the Busby Babes and what they gave to Manchester United. This is the 50th anniversary of the Munich Air Disaster, the accident that took their lives, so it's vital for the club to win this game. But fate has decided we're going to win this game. There's no way that we can lose this football match.'

I look at him. He's pushing 70 now, but I can't imagine him retiring from football. He lives for moments like this. People have been talking about him quitting United so he can put his feet up, but I know it isn't going to happen. Ronaldo and I are clicking in attack. Scholesy, Rio, Gary Neville and Giggsy are still going strong. I can tell he wants to work with us and mould another great team. Now we've won the league a couple of times, he's looking fitter and stronger than ever.

I've sussed that he wants to win the Champions League more than anything, because not winning it – like last year when we lost that semi-final against Milan – gives him a cob on. And in the dressing room or on the pitch he won't ever let us rest on our arses. Especially not tonight.

He tells us about the joys of winning the Champions League.

'There's no better feeling.'

He reminds us how lucky we are to be footballers.

'You don't know what hard work is,' he says. 'Your grand-parents worked hard every day just to get by. You've got 90 minutes to work hard and to win one football match and you're paid a lot of money to do it, so make sure you work. If you don't, I'll bring you off.'

He tells us about the poverty in Russia. He tells us that the grandparents of Russia's footballers and their fans had to work in industrial factories for a living. Then he tells us how privileged we are and how we shouldn't take anything for granted. It doesn't sound like much, but it's emotional stuff. His team talks really get to me sometimes. It makes me want to run harder, play better.

I'm desperate to get out there now.

How he handles this dressing room is important to the players, especially in big matches like this one. Some fans think he's created an Us Versus Them mentality in here. It's nothing like that at all. We know that the world isn't against us, but we do understand that everyone raises their game when they play United. Defenders tackle harder, wingers leg it faster, away fans boo us louder.

I know it's going to be so much harder in a Champions League final.

*****

It's funny, once I'm on the pitch, lined up against Chelsea in the Luzhniki Stadium in Moscow, history and other people's memories fly out of the window.

I want to make my own history.

Cameras start flashing all around us. Moscow is split down the middle with the two sets of fans, red and blue. Then I see the trophy on a podium on the pitch. It looks unbelievable. My heart is banging. I hear the fanfare of the Champions League music and I know tonight might be my only chance of playing in a game like this.

Remember what The Manager said, Wayne: 'No regrets.'

*****

It's chucking it down with rain.

The pitch is wet, which means the ball is zipping about, and the game starts well: we have a few chances on goal before Ronnie scores in the 26th minute, but we really should be out of sight already. We've dominated but we haven't taken our chances, so it doesn't shock me when we get punished. Chelsea score with just about the last kick of the half.

Sometimes a match changes in a second. Up until half-time we've been in control, but now we're walking to the dressing room on level terms. The mood has changed. Chances are, The Manager was planning on ordering us to play tight before the goal. Instead he tells us to go out and attack them again.

When we come out for the second half, I can feel the game slipping out of our control. It does my head in. We can't keep hold of the ball, Chelsea are winning every tackle. They hit the bar. As the clock runs down, I know we need to get to extra-time just to regroup and when we finally sit on the pitch after the final whistle, The Manager gets into us.

'You have to create more chances,' he says. 'If you don't, Chelsea will come on strong. You have to dig in.'

Extra-time is mentally and physically knackering for both teams. It's tense. We're tired and I'm limping.

My hip again.

Only my mind is keeping me going. It's the desire to win. I have to get my hands on that trophy. The thought of the prize at the end of the game is giving me the adrenaline, but it's not enough; my legs and lungs feel done in and The Manager soon sees that I'm finished, I'm exhausted, the battering I took from Ryan Nelsen is still killing me. My hip is hanging off. I've played through pain a few times this season and got away with it, but extra-time tonight is proving too much.

The board goes up.

The Manager subs me. I'm gutted, but I can sense that the team needs a fresh player, someone to take the game to Chelsea in the closing stages, and Nani, with all his skills, quick legs and trickery, takes my place. Suddenly Drogba slaps Vida and gets a red card, but despite the one-man advantage we've now got, it's not enough. After 90 minutes and extra-time, nothing separates us. It's a penalty shootout.

After the defeat to Arsenal in 2005, I hate penalty shootouts, just as much as the fans. It's a lottery. One mistake decides a final and makes a scapegoat out of whoever misses the deciding kick. And I'm in the worst possible situation: I'm a footy player who can't take a pen. I can't do my bit; I'm a supporter again. Just a lad like the rest of the fans in the ground watching from the sidelines, or the people drinking in a bar at home. And like those supporters, I know that the Champions League final is resting on the nerves of Ronnie, Carlos, Owen Hargreaves, Nani and Michael Carrick.

I want to take one.

When the shootout starts, we score two (Carlos, Carrick), they score two (Michael Ballack, Juliano Belletti); then the unbelievable happens. Ronaldo misses his kick.

He was our home banker!

Chelsea score two more; Hargreaves and Nani score for us. Everyone looks worried.

I watched England go out to Argentina on penalties in France 1998. I hated it. Bloody hell, the nerves now are just as bad as they were for me as a fan.

John Terry jogs up to take their fifth kick; his pen can win the game. Scoring the deciding goal in a Champions League final seems destined for JT. He's their captain, a hero to the Chelsea lot. I've watched him take penalties in England training sessions and I've never seen him miss once.

It's not going to be our night. Again.

He shapes to shoot right, sending Edwin to the ground, then he fires the ball the other way. It's a certain goal if he makes a sweet connection, but at the last second he slips. His standing foot goes out from underneath him and JT spoons his shot wide.

I jump up and celebrate. JT's an England teammate but right now, I don't care, I'm dead chuffed at his mistake.

That's the selfish streak that goes through every player when they're competing. He's sitting on the turf, head bowed, gutted. I'm cheering my head off.

It's a deciding moment and now I know we're going to win. The game is level on paper – 4–4; we've taken the same number of penalties – but psychologically, we're one-up. It's all coming down to bottle and our team has loads of it.

Anderson steps up: scores.

Salomon Kalou steps up: scores.

I wish I could be out there taking the next one for the team, but instead I'm here with The Manager, the coaches and the kit man. We're all watching as a season's work is decided on pens.

Giggsy steps up.

God knows what's going through his head. He's got so much experience that most of the time he never seems freaked out by big occasions. Tonight he looks composed, like he's playing in a training ground session and we're practising with a reserve goalie.

Giggsy scores.

Now it's Chelsea's turn to feel gutted. The game swings the other way.

Nicolas Anelka makes the long, lonely walk from the centre circle to the penalty area. I watch him go, but something's not right. It's his body language. He doesn't look confident. He's bricking it. I can see the fear in him and I want it to break him. I want the fear to make him slip like JT. I want him to scuff his shot, to blaze the ball over the bar.

Our fans are whistling; their fans are applauding every slow, cautious step. He puts the ball down. His face says he's beaten already. I know at this moment I'm going to get my hands on the Champions League trophy.

He takes his run up.

Miss.

He plants his standing foot, head down.

Miss. Hoof it over.

He strikes the ball sweetly, towards the left post, the ball curling just inside. It's at a height that always seems perfect for goalkeepers and Edwin gets down to it quickly. He saves, the ball ricocheting off his fist.

We've done it!

Everything goes blurry, mad. I'm racing towards the goal with Rio, Nani, Anderson, the coaches. Our fans are going nuts, I'm going nuts. Everyone's lost it. Ronaldo is laying on the grass, shaking with tears; JT is laying on the grass shaking with tears. I can see Gary Nev running over to him in the chucking rain, in his suit, to console him. He's a top lad, Gary.

I look at JT and decide to keep a lid on the celebrations in front of him. Sometimes football rolls for you, sometimes it doesn't. We're players for United, they're players for Chelsea but we're teammates for England and it's tough to see my teammates hurting; I'm not going to get in their faces about it right now. I'm just happy it isn't me sitting there.

I look up into the stadium to see Coleen and my family. There are thousands and thousands of fans smiling, laughing, people waving back. They're in there somewhere. Then I hear a Scouse accent next to me.

'Here, Wazza, she's up there,' says the voice.

When I turn around there's a lad I used to know from Crocky. He's stood next to me in a photographer's bib. Somehow he's blagged his way in. Before I can ask him how he got here, I spot them. I can see my family smiling and waving in the crowd, bursting with pride. Then I remember that losing a final on a penalty shootout is probably the worst feeling in football. Winning one is probably the best.

*****

We don't get to the celebration party until gone two in the morning. All the lads are there, having a few beers. Then The Manager gets up for another speech. He's just watched us win the Premier League and the Champions League, but now he's talking about next season, how we have to do it again. I look around at the lads and I can tell everyone's thinking the same thing.

Doesn't he ever switch off?

CHAPTER
12
DEBUT

In the summer holidays, a few weeks after the end of the season, a fan on holiday asks me about the Premier League titles, the League Cup and Champions League winner's medal; the battles with Chelsea, Arsenal and Liverpool: where did it all start? How come I managed to become a footy player? We have a chat, I crack on about how it all began on a tarmac football pitch behind my house. The Goals we called it, a tiny patch of land owned by a local youth club called The Gems.

I tell him that I was six when I went in there for the first time. I didn't stop going until I was 12. Every night after school I was out on that pitch, sometimes on my own, banging a ball against the chain-link fence and controlling the rebounds; hitting volleys and free-kicks from the halfway line, dribbling around imaginary defenders. It was the perfect size for one lad – basically a five-a-side pitch – and I could run from one end to the other pretty quickly with a footy at my feet.

If I wasn't practising my shooting, I'd stand in one corner of the pitch and play a diagonal pass to the other end. I'd do it with my instep and the outstep of my boot. I'd do it left foot, right foot. I'd dribble with the ball, trying stepovers and tricks. I wouldn't leave until Mum called me in for tea.

When The Gems closed for the evening, I'd bunk over the fence and play in The Goals for longer. The owners didn't mind. Sometimes I was out there so late, the caretaker of the building would even leave the floodlights on, especially for me. The first time it happened – the lights shining down, making those long shadows you see in an evening game in Europe – I felt like a proper footballer from the telly.

When I wasn't in my Everton shirt, playing footy, I used to go to the youth club as well. They had snooker tables and table tennis. I did dancing there. It was a great place because it gave the kids in the area somewhere safe to hang around. I loved it. Me and my mates could go there and have a laugh without getting into any trouble. It was open every night, so most evenings after school I'd be at The Gems, listening to music or playing snooker.

Most of the time, though, I was kicking a ball around the tarmac pitch. I'd imagine I was playing for Everton, I'd imagine I was Duncan Ferguson scoring goals in front of the Gwladys Street End at Goodison Park.

The Goals felt like my space. I felt privileged to be able to play there. If it hadn't been for that pitch, I probably wouldn't have developed as a footballer in the same way; I would have been different somehow. Playing there every night gave me the skills and the confidence to go up against opponents when I played for my school teams and Liverpool Schoolboys, or local sides like Copplehouse Colts, where I was first spotted by Liverpool and then Everton, who I later went on to sign pro forms with.

As a kid I always wanted to score goals, whoever I played for, but I was a midfielder for a little bit when I was younger, probably because I was skilful and could pass the ball well. It didn't stop me from getting in the box though. I scored loads from the middle of the park. Later, when I was pushed upfront, I scored even more goals. Scoring and winning was everything to me, even then. It's what the game's all about. If a footy player doesn't like scoring goals, there's something wrong with him (or her).

When I was a kid, I didn't really model myself on any one player. There was Duncan Ferguson, of course, because he had heart, but I was a big fan of Alan Shearer and Paul Gascoigne. Gazza had skill and imagination, but Shearer had everything: strength, technique, heading ability, and leadership. I buzzed off watching him play for England. He was the player I most wanted to be back then.

If a spectacular goal was scored at the weekend, I'd spend *my* weekend trying to recreate it, trying to pull off the same technique. I remember Tony Yeboah scored a blinding volley for Leeds against Liverpool in 1995. It dipped over the keeper and crashed into the back of the net like a bullet. For a week I spent hours hitting the ball towards the goal at The Gems in the same style. The same happened when Michael Owen scored that mazy goal for England in the 1998 World Cup against Argentina – I tried it in games until my manager and teammates started getting angry with me, telling me to pass, to lay it off to another lad in the team because I was hogging the ball too much.

Playing in The Goals started my career, but if someone had told me then that the end result would be me playing for Everton in the Premier League, Man United in the Champions League, and that I'd be the Premier League's youngest scorer (for a while), I'd never have believed them. It's something I could never have imagined happening to me, as much as I wanted it.

When it did, it was down to The Goals. That's where the skills in my game first came together.

*****

I tell the fan about my first game for Everton. How mad it was. I'd been playing footy with the club for a few years; when I signed professionally I was getting £75 a week at first, which was probably a lot less than some of my pals from Crocky. They were working on building sites for loads more money, but then I was playing footy every day with the likes of Big Dunc, Kevin Campbell and Steve Watson. I wouldn't have swapped places with them, no way.

I remember I used to see Gazza all the time when I was a youth team player. I loved watching him around the training ground. He was loud, always up to something. There was one time when I was 16, sitting in the dressing room before a youth team game. Gazza came in and let on to all of us as we got changed.

'Alright lads,' he goes. 'Any of you lot going out tonight?'

Everyone looked at one another. Everyone was thinking the same thing: *What's he up to?* In the end, I had to say something.

'Yeah, I am.'

Gazza got out his wallet and handed me two £20 notes.

'Here you go pal,' he said. 'Have a nice night on me.' I looked down at the money. None of the other lads could believe it – I'd just got a pay bonus off one of the greatest English midfielders ever.

When I moved up and started training with the first team it was weird, but only because I didn't get overawed or star struck, even though I was an Evertonian, a proper fan. I felt that I was already good enough to mix it with the other players (that Scouse confidence again); the senior lads always helped me to feel part of the side. Whenever I travelled with the first team to games during the pre-season campaign of 2002/03, I'd play computer games with Duncan Ferguson in his hotel room. It was brilliant.

Then, 24 hours before the season started, the manager, David Moyes, told me I was starting the game against Spurs at Goodison. I couldn't believe it, my debut was actually going to happen. He called me into his office and sat me down.

'Wayne, you're starting tomorrow,' he said. 'But I don't want you telling anyone apart from your parents. I don't want Spurs knowing before kick-off.'

So I went home and had to keep my mouth shut. I told my mum and dad, I called Coleen, but that was it. I wasn't allowed to tell anyone else. It was my cousin's birthday party down the road that night and I couldn't go. Instead I had to hang around the house while Mum made excuses for me. When I crashed out for the night I couldn't sleep because I was dead excited. I was walking around the house on my own; I was tossing and turning all night. I'd wake up every hour and look at the clock, praying for it to be morning, but it seemed to take forever.

At 7.30 a.m. I was up, dead keen, but there were still hours and hours to kill before I could leave for the game. I sat around the house and forced myself to relax. I looked at the clock: 8.11. I watched *Soccer AM* and looked at the clock: 9.32. At midday, Mum made my pre-match meal of chicken and baked beans and I looked at the clock again: 12.11. I swear the hands were moving in reverse, time seemed to be going that slowly. When it got to about one o'clock, it was time to get my kit bag, just as I had done for years and years playing Sunday league football and youth team games for Everton. But this time the stakes were a lot higher.

My Everton debut; Premier League football.

Dad drove me to the ground because I wasn't old enough to drive myself. I wasn't even old enough to drink, I was that young. He'd grown up an Everton fan and was so excited as we made our way to Goodison. Overexcited probably.

Normally all the players parked their cars in the players' car park, but Dad dropped me right at the main entrance of the ground, where all the directors walked in. I suppose we both went off to prepare for the game in our own way: I went into the ground and got changed, he went home, got a taxi to the pub and met his mates before the match. He was bursting with pride.

When I got into the dressing room and met up with the lads, I was excited, too. I felt ready. I'd believed in myself for so long and I knew I was good enough; I knew I should have been starting that game and when I saw my shirt hanging on the wall, it really hit home.

Rooney.

18.

Gazza's old shirt number.

As I started to prepare myself, David Moyes came over for a chat.

'Go out there and enjoy it, Wayne,' he said. 'Just relax and express yourself in the game.'

I focused myself; I looked around to take it all in. I could see that the other lads were up for it because it was the first match of the season. Everyone had been working so hard in the summer and we were desperate to make a good start. The funny thing was, they couldn't wait for the game to kick-off, but I couldn't wait for the *warm-up*. Everything was so new to me that even running around in a bib and stretching in front of the supporters was exciting. I was working with players that I had cheered from the seats. Now it was my turn to understand how an Everton player felt before a match. When I ran out onto the pitch for my Premier League start, the home fans gave me a massive cheer. I was a local lad and they wanted me to do well. I didn't want to let them down.

*****

A mad thing happened as I kicked a ball around before the start of the match: I imagined I was back in The Goals. I ran onto the pitch and saw them as clear as day. I was firing shots towards our keeper Richard Wright, warming up in front of the fans, and to calm the nerves I imagined I was back at home, shooting at the rusty goal frames and torn netting behind the old youth club. It got my head set for the game.

Everything felt so exciting; the supporters were dead pleased to see me play. I suppose some of them had watched me on the telly in the FA Youth Cup games – we got to the final the previous season but lost to Villa. There was a lot of talk in the local press and the national papers about me. The supporters had noticed me on the bench at the end of the 2001/02 campaign and must have wondered what sort of player I was going to become, but I reckon they were more chuffed that a real Evertonian had made it into the first team.

I was one of them.

As the game kicked off, I could hear the fans singing my name. I got my first touch and everyone cheered. Spurs were a great team to play against and they had some top players at the time, like Teddy Sheringham, Les Ferdinand and

Jamie Redknapp, but I wasn't going to let that overawe me. I loved getting stuck in. I remember Tottenham got a corner and as I went back to the edge of the box, Sheringham started arguing with one of our players. I said something to him, even then. I was a kid, he was a 30-something England international with goals in European Championships; he had a Champions League winner's medal from his time with United, but I wasn't afraid to speak my mind.

After 67 minutes, I knew I'd played alright, but the manager brought me off – I think he thought I was going to wear myself out. I was upset, I wanted to stay on, but the fans gave me a standing ovation. They wanted me to know that I'd done my bit to get us a 2–2 draw. Meanwhile, I'd felt the buzz of playing Premier League football for the first time and I wanted more, much more.

*****

After the match my dad went to the local ale house for a couple of pints like he always did. I went in to see him for a chat about the game. The fans in the pub couldn't believe it when I walked in. They were made up for me, coming over to say hello, wishing me luck for the rest of the season. Everyone was proud that a lad from Crocky had come through at such a young age, they were delighted for me. I sat there with my can of pop, trying to take it all in.

Bloody hell, I guess I'm a Premier League player now.

*****

My first two goals came against Wrexham in the Worthington Cup and, yeah, it was great to score for the Everton first team, but I wasn't as excited as I thought I'd be because it was the Worthington Cup and I wanted to score in the Premier League. I had it in my head that I could get a goal in the league before I reached the age of 17. Thankfully, I didn't have to wait that long for it.

Arsenal, 19 October 2002, the last game before my birthday.

The match was at Goodison. I was a sub that day, but the one thing I remember more than anything was seeing the Arsenal players lining up in the tunnel before the match. I spotted Sol Campbell, David Seaman and Patrick Vieira. Thierry Henry and Kanu were there. All of them were huge. I'd never realised just how big David Seaman was. I'd seen him on the TV loads, but when I stood next to him I thought, *Wow, he's massive.*

They seemed to loom over us in footballing terms as well. Freddie Ljungberg scored for them just seven minutes into the game; our striker, Tomasz Radzinski equalised 15 minutes later. I was desperate to get on. I was watching the Arsenal back four from the bench and I noticed that when-ever any of our players got the ball in behind their midfield, their centre-halves would drop off a lot. *I thought: If I can get into that space I'll have a go at goal.*

Then, in the second half, the boss gave me a nod.

'Get warmed up, Wayne,' he said. 'You're going on.'

I looked up at the clock; there was only 10 minutes to go, but I was delighted to be getting a run-out because

Arsenal were a quality side. They were top of the table and unbeaten for 30 league games. I wanted to try myself out against the best.

Then, in the 90th minute I scored the winning goal.

The ball got played up and midfielder Thomas Gravesen got a touch. The ball bounced over to me and I brought it down. Suddenly I was in that space between Arsenal's defence and midfield and I stuck to my promise.

Sol Campbell has backed off, I'm having this.

I took a touch and whipped the ball as hard as I could, curling it towards the near post. It left my toes and whizzed past Seaman who was standing on his line, the ball smashing the underside of the bar and bouncing down behind him. There was nothing he could have done to stop that one.

I've scored!

I went mad, I ran to the fans; it felt amazing, incredible. I could see the faces on the supporters and I knew then that I'd done something special for them. God knows what must have been going through Dad's mind, but when the game ended and I sat in the dressing room, 20 minutes after the final whistle had blown, I could still hear the crowds singing my name in the streets outside Goodison Park.

*****

After the game I went into the pub with my dad. The locals were all over me. Then I went to Coleen's house and played footy with my mates in the garages around the back of her house, like I always did on a Saturday. It was dark. The streetlights were shining down onto the scrap of land where we were playing. I'd just scored the winning goal for Everton against Arsenal, but I was still kicking the ball about with the lads from home like it was as important as 90 minutes in the Premier League. That was my way of celebrating. It's mad I know, but all I wanted to do was play football back then.

CHAPTER

13

MANCHESTER

The funny thing is, chatting to that lad on holiday got me thinking about the type of player I'd become, the type of footballer I was when I was a lad.

When I first started playing for Everton, I was dead raw. I was a hothead. I'd always lose my rag if things weren't going well for me and in my first season I picked up eight yellow cards and one red. The first sending off was horrible. I came on as a sub against Birmingham City and picked up a pass, turned and ran at their defence. My touch let me down, it was too heavy, and as I tried to reclaim the ball, I lunged in for it as their centre-half Steve Vickers cleared it away. I couldn't stop myself in time and I went through him, my studs cutting into his shin (the gash was so bad he needed 10 stitches afterwards, which I felt terrible about). I never meant to catch him; I was genuinely trying to get the ball. The ref didn't see it that way though and showed me the red card.

The walk to the dressing room was a nightmare. The tunnel at Birmingham was in the far corner of the ground and it was miles away. The tackle had taken place in probably the furthest point away on the pitch and it took me ages to get there. All the Birmingham fans were giving it as I trudged back. When I got inside, it was the coldest dressing room ever, it was freezing. And sitting in there on my own gave me too much time to think – I was devastated because I knew that I'd have to miss the next three games.

At that time in my life, the flare-ups happened because of the adrenaline, the excitement that took me over whenever I got onto a footy pitch in front of thousands of fans. Everything was so exciting then that it was hard not to get carried away whenever I pulled on an Everton shirt. I remember clashing with the West Brom defender Darren Moore when we played them in the league. I was running down the wing, he was chasing after me. I stopped the ball dead; I could see that he didn't want to come in too close to me in case I moved the ball past him. Instead he waited, standing off, so I put a foot on the ball – my hands on my hips – as he jockeyed me, forcing me to make a move. I could see he was thinking, 'The cheeky git' and when I poked the ball past him and moved away, he tackled me hard. I was being disrespectful, so I deserved it I suppose.

I could get above myself off the pitch as well. I hated being dropped. After a couple of games in the team, David

Moyes named me as a sub and I was fuming afterwards; I sulked around the house when I heard the news. Thinking about it now, I can see that he wanted to save me, to stop me from burning out, but I wanted to play and there was nothing the management team or the other players in the squad could do to cheer me up if I was out of the side. They knew the way I was, that I hated to back down or to be second best, and it was probably for that reason that he later dropped me for the Merseyside derby at Anfield, a 0–0 draw. I think the manager thought I was going to lose my head, especially as I was an Evertonian and the game meant so much more to me than some of the other players.

I was upset again. Moody. I sat in the dressing room before the game, gutted that I couldn't play. I made the walk down the tunnel and saw their famous 'This Is Anfield' sign (it meant nothing to me); I wanted to get a result for our side of the city. As I got out to the bench I knew most of my family would be at home watching the results coming in on the telly. Most of them hadn't come to the ground – some of them hated Liverpool so much they wouldn't dream of going to Anfield for the derby, and I was desperate to make my mark for them. When I finally got on in the second half I thumped a shot against the bar. Later, when the ball was played in over the top, I ran through the Liverpool back four as their keeper, Chris Kirkland, raced out for the ball. We both went for it 100% and smashed into one another, the pair of us hitting the deck with a thump. My hip was throbbing. The physio raced on.

'You alright, Wayne?'

'Yeah, fine.'

I was lying. I was in agony. But there was no way I was limping off the field in a Merseyside derby at Anfield.

*****

I took it all in my stride. The biggest stadiums, the biggest players, an England debut against Australia in 2003. I didn't stop to think about how huge it all was. I was ready; I felt like I could do anything. Looking back now I can see how special the adventure had become, but at the time, I just wanted to be playing.

The money was crazy too. I was still on £75 a week; I'd just turned 17. Then the club gave me a professional footballer's wage, an amount I couldn't have even imagined earning when I was at school. When my first payslip came through, I couldn't believe the numbers. The funny thing was, I had to wait another month before the money went into my account, so I borrowed a bit of cash from Mum to tide me over. When payday arrived, it felt weird. I'd never seen money like that in my bank account before.

Everton finished just outside the European places in 2002/03, and to celebrate my first season I took Coleen to Miami for a holiday. We were so young; it was our first time abroad. We sat on the plane in first class and the stewards brought us some complimentary champagne. We were excited and ordered a couple of drinks, then Coleen knocked a glass off the table into my lap and I had to spend the rest of the flight half-naked, an airline blanket wrapped around my waist as my pants were dried by the stewards. We were like little kids back then and everything was so new, even our first holiday away together.

*****

Everton weren't good enough the following season, I'm not sure why exactly; I think some of it was down to the fact that we were an ageing team. There were a lot of players coming to the end of their careers as 2003/04 got underway – Duncan, Alan Stubbs, Scott Gemmill, Mark Pembridge, David Weir and David Unsworth. It was always going to be a difficult year. We weren't good enough as a team and the standard of football and the way we played was disappointing. We finished 17th, one place above the relegation zone.

By the end of the campaign I knew I could play for one of the bigger sides in the Premier League because I had become a first-team regular for England, lining up alongside Steven Gerrard, David Beckham, Frank Lampard and Paul Scholes. All of them were great players and I had fitted in just fine. At the time I was probably playing as well as any of those names, especially after the European Championships in 2004 where I scored four goals. After that tournament I didn't have any doubts that I could play at the highest level – at a club challenging for the Premier League title or the Champions League.

The rumours about me leaving Everton started at around the same time. In January 2004, the papers made out that Chelsea, United, Arsenal and Newcastle wanted to sign me.

I didn't know how true those rumours were, but I was happy that other teams had taken notice of what I was doing. After the Euros, I made up my mind to leave Goodison Park.

One of the teams apparently chasing me was Real Madrid. As the talking became more serious, I decided that I'd be happy to play in Spain, but only if Man United didn't come in for me – they were always my number one choice. I actually spoke to my mum and dad and Coleen about it. They said, 'Whatever you decide, we'll be right behind you,' but to be honest, my heart was hoping for a move to Old Trafford rather than Spain.

In the end it was Newcastle who made the first bid at £20 million, but Everton turned it down. Then United put their offer in. I sat down with David Moyes and told him I wanted to go to Old Trafford.

'Will you accept the bid from them?'

He felt that the money wasn't high enough but in the end United made a bigger offer. I went into his office and said, 'Listen, I've told you, I think it would be better if you accepted the offer. You know I love the club but for the sake of my career I want the opportunity to play at the highest level.'

He said, 'Unless you put a transfer request in, you're not leaving.'

I went straight into the club secretary's office and got her to draft a letter for me, asking to leave the club. Once it was printed off I went back into the manager's office.

'There you are,' I said. 'There's your transfer request. Will you accept United's offer?'

It was tough as an Everton fan to make that decision, but I felt that I had to take the opportunity and join United. A chance like that might never have come round again – I wanted to play at Old Trafford for my football career. I now understand David Moyes' position. He didn't want me to leave, I did. He wanted to make sure Everton Football Club got the best price they possibly could for me.

*****

It's funny how coincidences crop up in football. At the start of the 2004/05 campaign, the night before the transfer deadline day, Man United played Everton at Old Trafford. I was injured at the time, having busted my foot in Euro 2004. A section of the Man United fans were singing my name, which felt dead weird, and the Everton fans were understandably going mad. I probably would have signed that day if that game hadn't been taking place. In the end, the transfer went through at the last hour.

Despite the fuss, my head was quite sound. I felt alright, I didn't really think about the size of the deal, the money or the headlines. I was confident that I could play for Man United. More importantly, I was desperate to win trophies. Looking back, I made the right move.

CHAPTER
14
RIVALS

We're a month into the 2008/09 season. I lifted the Champions League trophy in Moscow a few months earlier, but the buzz is wearing off and I'm dead moody because Liverpool are sitting at the top of the Premier League along with Chelsea.

PREMIER LEAGUE TABLE, 13 SEPTEMBER 2008

	PLAYED	GD	POINTS
1/ CHELSEA	4	7	10
2/ LIVERPOOL	4	3	10
3/ ARSENAL	4	7	9

It's funny, but I can't shake the feeling that I had when I was a kid watching Everton in the stands with my dad: *I don't want to see Liverpool do well*. Even as a professional footballer I still have the same emotions I had as a young fan. Of course, I respect Liverpool as a football club. I respect the history they have and the trophies they've won, but I've grown up hating them because that's what football fans do and that feeling has never gone away. I even tell a journalist that I still hate Liverpool and all hell breaks loose in the papers. There are headlines:

'ROONEY: I HATE KOP'

The Manager has to put the press straight.

'Hate's an easy word to say, easier than dislike,' he says. 'Maybe it's not the right word. He's had a lot of stick from their fans over the years, so it's understandable.'

The thing is, I've been brought up that way. Most of my family – Evertonians all of them – won't even go to Anfield to watch the Merseyside derby because the divide is so big between the fans. They can't stand the place. But it works both ways. I reckon if I was to ask Steven Gerrard or Jamie Carragher about the rivalry – lads who play for Liverpool with a real passion for the club – they'd say the same thing about United or Everton. As supporters I think that's the way we've all been brought up. *It's tribal*.

Some people might think that's crazy, but as players that feeling, that *dislike*, doesn't go away, even for a bunch of grown men playing professionally for a Premier League club. I think the English lads who have grown up supporting a team will always feel that sense of rivalry.

It's different for the foreign lads. They've grown up supporting teams from their own countries, their football passions remain at home. A bit more energy and pride hits the English lads when they're tied up emotionally with teams in the Premier League, especially in derby matches. So, for me, it's not nice to see Liverpool flying out of the traps at the start of the season.

It doesn't help that we're a bit off the pace, too.

PREMIER LEAGUE TABLE, 13 SEPTEMBER 2008

	PLAYED	GD	POINTS
13/ UNITED	3	0	4

The reason for Liverpool's good start hinges on the partnership between Gerrard and their Spanish striker, Fernando Torres, who signed for the club in 2007. The pair of them have really clicked this year and they seem to be causing a lot of trouble for defenders. As an attacker, I can see that Torres is a brilliant player (it's all part of the Striker's Appreciation Society – I can suss the talent in other forwards, whoever they play for). He's hungry, he's quick, he has a good eye for goal.

I think Liverpool's style of play suits him, too. Torres thrives on really fast counter-attacking football and Liverpool get the ball forward quickly, whereas some teams – like Chelsea under their new manager, Luiz Felipe Scolari

177

– tend to build slowly from the back. At the moment they wouldn't suit the way that Torres plays, or the runs he makes into the box.

We sign a pretty good striker for ourselves, though: Dimitar Berbatov, the Bulgarian centre-forward who's had a couple of great seasons at Spurs. He joins at the end of the transfer window, right at the death, and he's a brilliant addition to the squad. I've watched him play on the telly quite a few times so I know just how good he can be on his day.

With his skill I also know it won't take Berba long to fit in, even though he's completely different to what we have in the squad – he likes to slow the ball down and take touches; he's unselfish. He's also a lot stronger than people think. In his first training session he shrugs away a few defenders in a scrap for a loose ball, which comes as a bit of a surprise.

Some say he's not the loudest off the pitch, and that he likes to keep himself to himself in the dressing room. I'm not bothered about how loud or funny he is. He's a fantastic player, and that's all that matters to me.

With the new arrival, it looks like The Manager will be spoilt for choice when it comes to picking his team. Myself, Ronnie, Carlos and Berba will all be fighting it out for two, maybe three places this season, but it's great for the club that we have so many strike options, and to be honest, it doesn't worry me. If anything, it gives me a determination to play better. It keeps me on my toes. I know I'll have to concentrate and work hard all the time this season. *If I don't, one of that lot will win my place.*

At first, The Manager sets the team up with me and Berba up front, Ronnie on the wing. He then changes it by playing just me up top in a 4–5–1 formation. Carlos finds himself sitting quite a few games out and, to be honest, I feel a bit bad for him (but not bad enough to ever let him take my place). He hasn't done a lot wrong, but he just can't break into the starting XI. That's the way football goes, I guess. It's about The Manager and the team he writes down before every game. The rest of us have to fall in line, and after that it's down to the players. As long as everyone scores goals and it helps us to win the title, we'll be fine.

As long as it helps us to knock Liverpool down a peg or two, I'll be happy.

*****

We get our act together ...

Chelsea 1 Manchester United 1
Manchester United 2 Bolton 0
Blackburn Rovers 0 Manchester United 2
Everton 1 Manchester United 1
Manchester United 2 West Ham 0
Manchester United 4 Hull City 3

It's not long before we're in third place. Right up Liverpool's backside.

*****

If anyone asks me what my favourite trophy is in football, I always say it's the Premier League, followed by the Champions League, followed by the FA Cup, and then the League Cup. Why? Well I've grown up with the Premier League. It's where I've always wanted to be, ever since I was a kid. Don't get me wrong, the Champions League is great, it's exciting, but the Premier League is the one I always want to win because week in, week out, I'm in the thick of it.

It takes me over.

I know the teams and the players, the managers and the stadiums – I see them on the box all the time. Then there's the physicality, the speed and the quality of the football. It's a different class. Everywhere, people are talking about it. The league dominates the papers, the fans read every word. *And the need to win the title is drilled into us by The Manager every single day.*

Some supporters might think, 'Oh there's so much money in the game, footballers don't really care about what competitions they play in. They don't care whether they win or lose.' That might be true for some players, but I don't think like that.

I didn't start playing football for money and it's not what drives me now.

Money obviously gives me a great way of living and it's helped me to raise a family in a way that makes me happy, but the cash is not everything for me. It's not the sole thing in my life. I'm happiest if United win things, I'm happiest if my family's happy. The money can add to that feeling, sure, but I'm not one of those lads who goes crazy every week, throwing my money around just to make myself feel better or to show off.

I do appreciate that footballers get a lot for what we do, but the club has set a wage for me, so that's what they must value me at. It's a competitive rate in line with other top teams so it works the same as any other business. And of course people ask me if we get too much money, but the honest answer is, *I don't know*. If that's the budget available to players in football at the top level (because of what the sponsors, investors and the TV companies spend on the Premier League) then it must be fair. I don't set the budgets.

There are lots of other sports that are better paid than football at the top level, but nobody seems to mind. If people were to look at the NBA or the NFL in America, the top golf pros, Formula One, they'd see that the biggest stars in those sports get much more than footballers in England do, but nothing gets said. It's the same as films: a lot of actors get paid much more than Premier League players, but nobody moans about them either, and they're in the entertainment business, just like us.

The important thing is, I'm grateful for everything that football has given me: the fun, the buzz of playing and, of course, the wealth, but I haven't lost touch with reality. I've bought nice cars and a house for myself and Coleen. I've even bought a place for my family, but I don't think that I've ever been over the top or madly extravagant. I'm just making the most of what football has given me and I'm dead grateful for it.

*****

As the season gets into full swing, I realise that money doesn't just change the way most fans think about players, it also changes the way they think about clubs.

City.

Suddenly they've got cash to spend having been taken over by the super rich Abu Dhabi United Group in the summer. They're talking about who they're going to buy and where the club is going to go in the next few years, which suddenly makes the Manchester derby this season a little bit spicier. They're chatting about titles and being the biggest club in the country, maybe Europe.

They're going to be a challenge to us from now on.

It's weird for me to see them up there, as a threat. I've been used to watching City finish way below United, ever since I fell in love with footy as a kid. They've always been miles away in the league despite the occasional win over us. Now it's great to have an extra edge to the games, some top of the table clashes. I don't know how The Manager views the takeover, but I do know that the players want to beat them more than ever. The fact that City are suddenly getting a little bit closer in terms of ambition gives us an extra incentive, a bigger desire to make sure we stay on top.

A bit more fight and battle is going to be needed to make sure that we keep ahead of the other lot.

I'm not sure how I feel when teams like City start throwing money around. As a player, I know there's nothing I can do about it; I know it's out of my hands. And I also know that United do it too sometimes, but that's the way football has gone. There's a lot of money in the game these days and every team is trying to improve their squad.

Nobody can blame a manager for wanting to bring better players into their club, like at City when the chairman is telling him to spend, spend, spend. That's only natural. But I do worry about the health of football, especially when I see big clubs going to the wall. There are teams falling into administration up and down the country every year now. I reckon it's important that clubs only spend money when they can, when they're financially secure. They shouldn't gamble the money or spend big when they're skint. I think they should always stay within their budget.

Mates who support other teams always say, 'Oh yeah, pal, it's easy for you, you play for Manchester United. Money isn't really an issue for your club.' That's a fair point, but even the players in our dressing room can see that football's a mad game. One year a team can be challenging for cups, the next they're in financial trouble, selling all their players and facing protests from the fans. These days, clubs should make sure they're only buying the players they can afford and they shouldn't break the bank to do it.

City can clearly afford anyone. The players and fans can see that their owners have loads to spend. We can tell that money will never stop with them, that they can splash anything on a player. But we'll have to forget about their money. *We have to dig in and work.*

*****

On 30 November we beat City, 1–0. I score the winner just before half-time. It's always sound to get a goal against them, especially today because there's a really moody atmosphere surrounding the game, but also because it shows the world that we're still on top.

In December we win our group in the Champions League; in the league we beat Sunderland, Stoke, Boro' and draw with Spurs at their place. We close the gap on Liverpool to seven points. *We have to dig in and work.*

*****

We have to dig in and work because I don't play for prestige. I play to win.

Being an expensive footballer hasn't helped me to win these games or added to my day-to-day life. To be honest, I don't think about my financial value as a player. I didn't even think about the transfer fee when I was sold to United by Everton, despite the big fuss that was made about it by everyone at the time. It was obviously a deal that the two clubs had struck, but I didn't think about the numbers being chucked about because they didn't seem real to me. At the time I was just thinking about playing and trying to win trophies at the highest level.

When we win trophies at United, I don't really celebrate or show off about it because showing off's not for me. I'm not one for big parties, not if I'm going to be the centre of attention anyway. I always remember when I scored my 100th goal for United. After the game I went home and watched TV; I called in a Chinese takeaway. A few of our lads went out that night and when I saw them the next day, I asked them where they'd been.

'Oh, so and so had a do because he'd made his 100th appearance for Man City.'

I couldn't get my head around that. Obviously some people don't need an excuse to have a party. I'd much rather go home and put my feet up.

And I definitely don't play football for the fame or to live a mad lifestyle.

I think footballers in this country are made out to be crazy superstars, but most of us are normal people. We get paid a lot of money for what we do, obviously, and we live a surreal life, but some fans think that we're up our own backsides. People say that footballers are disconnected from everyone else, but the simple fact is, I can't live my life like I used to when nobody knew me because it's impossible.

Fans want to have a go at me in the street. Photographers follow me around when I'm walking through the supermarket, doing the shopping. That's enough for me, cheers. Fans say, 'Why don't you go to the pub with the supporters like they did in the old days?' Or, 'Why do you hide away and not meet the public?' It's because doing that can cause me a lot of bother. And when it does, it's a 'mare.

I'm not trying to say, 'Oh poor me.' I don't want sympathy from anyone, I'm just telling it how it is. I know I have to take the rough with the smooth; the football and the money with the attention and abuse. It's just that I've learned that it's all about the game for me, not the pay cheque, the prestige, or the fame. When I think about what I'd like to leave behind when I retire, this is how it is for me:

1) I want to be thought of as somebody who gave everything every time he played.
2) I want to be thought of as a winner.
3) I want to be thought of as a striker that could score and create goals.
4) I want to be thought of as one of the best.
5) That's it. I reckon the most important thing for me is that the fans think of me as someone who works hard, someone that tries their hardest. I want to be thought of as being honest.

Honesty in football is tough. People think that football's easy, that the players don't have to put in the work to succeed. I'm not like that. I hate the thought of not putting a shift in, and I hate it when I see footballers not pulling their weight. I've known players to go missing during games against us, especially when their team's been losing 1–0 or 2–0.

They give up. I've seen strikers hiding behind our defenders with their arms up, pretending to want the ball, making out to the fans that they're dead keen to change the game. Deep down they know that the pass won't come to them, that the winger has pushed the ball too far to make a cross at the byline. *That they'll get away with it.*

That's not for me and I hope the fans realise it. Like my mum and dad taught me: *The best quality in life is to work hard*. But grafting – especially under pressure – is probably the toughest thing in life and in football. It's a skill to be able to do it and to do it well. And it takes bravery, because if I make a mistake and it costs United the game, there's nowhere to hide. Not in the Premier League.

When the final whistle has blown and we've lost a game, I don't think about the money. I think about the defeat. And it always does my head in.

*****

By January, Liverpool are still top of the league. I know I won't be able to take it if that lot nick the Premier League off us. If that happens, all the money in the world won't make my bad mood go away.

CHAPTER
15
FACT!

A January afternoon. I'm sitting at the kitchen table at home, aching from a morning's training session. *Sky Sports News* on the telly, the sound turned down. All of a sudden the cameras cut to Liverpool. The manager, Rafa Benitez, is about to give a press conference. Nothing strange about that, it'll be the usual chat about injuries, most probably; suspensions, some January transfer window stuff. But hang on, Rafa's pulling out a scrap of paper from his pocket as he starts addressing the journalists in the room.

What's going on here? Is he jacking it in?

I grab the controls and turn the sound up.

'… I think they are nervous because we are at the top of the table …'

He's talking about us.

'… During the Respect campaign – and this is a fact – Mr Ferguson was charged by the FA for improper conduct after comments made about [referee] Martin Atkinson and [ex referee] Keith Hackett. He was not punished. He is the only manager in the league that cannot be punished for these things …'

What's he banging on about here?

I walk closer to the box. Rafa's still reading from his scrap of paper.

'If he wants to talk about fixtures, and have a level playing field – as you say in England – (then) there are two options if we don't want more problems with fixtures. One is the same as in Spain, (where) the draw for the first part of the league is known, everyone knows which weekend (they are playing). In the second half everyone plays the opposite, so you all know. Sky and Setanta have the right to choose their games and it will be the same for everyone. So Mr Ferguson will not be complaining about fixtures and a campaign against United.

'Or there is another option. That Mr Ferguson organises the fixtures in his office and sends it to us and everyone will know and cannot complain. That is simple.'

Eh? Don't be soft …

'We know what happens every time we go to Old Trafford (with) the United staff. They are always going man-to-man with the referees, especially at half-time when they walk close to the referees and they are talking and talking …'

He's on a flippin' roll now.

'... All managers need to know is that only Mr Ferguson can talk about the fixtures, can talk about referees and nothing happens. We need to know that I am talking about facts, not my impression. There are things that everyone can see every single week ...'

I can't believe it.

Facts, my backside.

The people at Sky flash the Premier League up on the screen.

Proper facts.

PREMIER LEAGUE TABLE, 9 JANUARY 2009

	PLAYED	GD	POINTS
1/ LIVERPOOL	20	22	45
2/ CHELSEA	20	31	42
3/ UNITED	18	19	38

Well, Liverpool are seven points clear of us (though we've got two games in hand) and I know that, right now, they should be focusing on the second half of the season – the business end. Instead, their manager is talking, moaning about fixture issues and referees to the press. He's reading out a list of so-called 'facts' about how United apparently hassle the league's refs, and how we moan about the fixtures. At this very moment I think: *Liverpool probably won't win the league because The Manager has got under Rafa's skin; we've got under Liverpool's skin.*

And also, it's a load of rubbish.

Everyone knows Rafa's clutching at straws here. The fans and the Premier League officials won't fall for any of this stuff, surely? Maybe he wants to intimidate the Premier League's refs into giving decisions against us? Maybe he wants to turn the media against us? I'm not sure. What I do know is that his players will be disappointed when they get together at training tomorrow. I know I would be if I was playing for them. If there's going to be any damage caused by Rafa's rant on the box then it won't be inflicted on United. It'll hurt Liverpool Football Club and their players instead.

It'll backfire.

They're losing it.

We'll be fired up after this.

*****

The next day, The Manager doesn't mention Rafa Benitez to anyone at the training ground because he doesn't have to. Everyone's talking about it. And we're all laughing.

'The best thing was the sheet of paper with his notes on!' shouts one of the lads in the dressing room.

'He's gone too far ...,' says another.

But when The Manager gets into us on the pitch – working us hard in a practice game – the laughing and the joking stops pretty quickly. It's business as usual. No one's talking about Rafa's facts anymore because The Manager wants us to concentrate. He knows we're all fired up, that the psychological edge is with us, and that the important thing is to focus tactically.

He's obviously built up a lot of experience when dealing with situations like these over the years, especially at the end of the season when every point seems vital. And while I'm not sure if he genuinely likes getting involved in mind games with other gaffers, I do know that he's good at it. When other coaches try to unsettle United, or unsettle him, he's so experienced that he can switch those tactics around. He can put pressure back on another team with a sharp sentence in a press conference or post-match interview, which is obviously a great help for us when it comes to winning league titles. The fans only have to look at what happened to Kevin Keegan and Newcastle in 1995/96 when The Manager rattled them.

The edge is with us now.

Rafa's done his job for him.

We can win the league again …

*****

We smash Chelsea 3–0 and the result strengthens our position in third place.

We beat Wigan 1–0. I score in the first minute to push us into second.

When Berba scores in the 90th minute to win the game against Bolton for us 1–0, we go to the top of the table. Everton, West Ham, Fulham, Blackburn and Newcastle are all taken down before we meet Liverpool at Old Trafford on 14 March. We've already lost to this lot at Anfield earlier in the season (2–1), but that's because their place is always a tough ground to go to for any team, anything can happen. But this time, at Old Trafford …

We get well and truly battered.

We start well, Ronaldo scores a penalty, but then the wheels fall off and Liverpool respond by scoring four. Vida gets a red card and Torres runs us ragged as we push them in an attempt to score goals. They pick us off on the break and when we sit down in the dressing room afterwards, licking our wounds, The Manager looks a bit shocked. He can't believe we've been beaten 4–1. There's silence. Nobody moves for half an hour. It's horrible.

*****

The night before the Pompey game, April; United still top of the league. Because I'm sent off in the 2–0 defeat at Craven Cottage (when the ref thinks I've thrown the ball at him), I miss the 3–2 win over Villa and the 2–1 victory at Sunderland. By the time I come back into the starting XI, the whole squad are readying themselves for another massive game: Pompey at home, a midweek match.

As always, the team gets together in a Manchester hotel on the night before the game and we're shut away from the world. Downstairs in the hotel bar, the evening is going on as normal for everyone else: a gang of people are having their work night out; fans are here from all over the country for the game. Some lads are obviously going to a fancy dress party and are waiting for a taxi in the foyer. One of them is dressed as Dracula.

We're totally cut off up here. Most of the guests in the restaurant downstairs probably haven't got a clue that there's a squad of Premier League players staying at the hotel because everything we do tonight takes place away from the public. Dinner and team meetings happen in function rooms where nobody can see or disturb us. If we watch a late game as a team on the telly, it's done in a suite well away from the other guests, or in our bedrooms. It's the same deal week in, week out. Everyone knows tomorrow night is a big match, so the trick is to keep the routine as normal, and as peaceful, as possible.

Footballers are funny about routine. We want our time-tables and schedules to stay the same before every game. Team dinners, meetings, coach journeys: the routine can't be messed with. I need to know exactly what I'm doing and at what time. That way I can get my body and mind right. I need to know when to relax. I need to know when to eat my tea. I need to know when to sleep.

What I really want to know, though, is where everyone's going to watch the Liverpool v Arsenal game which is being shown on the telly. I wander down to a bedroom where the physios are working on Michael Carrick, Edwin van der Sar and Jonny Evans. Everyone's lounging around, their eyes fixed on the plasma screen where the game is playing. Next door, Berba is watching the match on his own, sat on the edge of his bed like a fan.

For the next 90 minutes it's a cracking game. Liverpool have to win if they're to put any pressure on us in the title race and it's an end-to-end match. Goal after goal flies in.

Arsenal's latest signing, Andrei Arshavin, a Russian striker, is having an absolute blinder, he's scored a hat-trick. The score is poised at 3–3 in the 90th minute and …

Bloody hell! He's only gone and got a fourth!

The whole room goes mental. Everyone starts jumping on Edwin van der Sar who's having his back rubbed; Berba starts banging on the wall, he's shouting and cheering in his room next door. We're all jumping around the gaff like little kids, like we've scored the goal ourselves.

In the celebrations we almost miss the fact that Liverpool pull the game level in the dying seconds, but who cares? A draw is no good for them tonight, they're at home.

We're one step closer to winning the title and we haven't even kicked a ball in anger.

*****

The following morning I look at the newspapers. The Premier League table tells me that we're joint top with Liverpool on 71 points, but we've still got two games in hand. Two games we have to win.

*****

After the draw with Arsenal, Liverpool fall away in the league; we go until the end of the season unbeaten:

Pompey, 2–0
Spurs, 5–2

Boro', 2–0
City, 2–0
Wigan, 2–1
Arsenal, 0–0
Hull, 1–0

FINAL PREMIER LEAGUE TABLE 2008/09

	PLAYED	GD	POINTS
1/ UNITED	38	44	90
2/ LIVERPOOL	38	50	86
3/ CHELSEA	38	44	83

Winning the Premier League this year is extra special because it means we've matched Liverpool's league titles in the football history books. To win any title is great, but to win an 18th, a feat that puts us level with them (while beating them to the league at the same time), is a special feeling for us all at the club, but as an Everton fan, it feels dead satisfying. It would have been a nightmare to have seen Liverpool win the league; I don't think Evertonians or the Manchester United fans would have heard the last of it, not for a long while.

Least of all, me.

I'm finding that winning these trophies isn't enough though. Once I've got a trophy, I'm always thinking about the next because I want to win more. I don't even look at my medals after I've won them. I haven't picked any of them up since I put them away in a room in one corner of the house.

I don't know why. I know I never want to lose them, but I've never got them together, admired them and thought, *Wow, I've got a Premier League winner's medal or a Champions League medal.* Maybe that's because I'm desperate to win more, or maybe I'm just dead greedy.

*****

In April and May, we play Arsenal in the Champions League semi-final over two legs, having beaten Inter and Porto in the knockout stages. Some players might think that the sparkle goes out of a European tie when two English teams are drawn together, but that isn't the case at all for me. I love it, there's a real edge to the game. The build-up is bigger in the papers and on the telly. The fans are really up for it; the whole country gets hyped up.

It's a different style of game from a Premier League match too, because away goals count and that really changes the mood, tactically at least. In the first leg at Old Trafford, we score against Arsenal first and then sit back. The Manager doesn't want us to concede an away goal, whereas in the league we'd probably push for a second. We eventually win 1–0 and in the second leg at The Emirates we score early on. Suddenly, we're in the driving seat.

I love games like this. We've got an away goal in the bag and a two-goal cushion overall. Arsenal have to score three to win. I know they'll come at us and attack, which means that gaps will open up in front of me as their midfield pushes forward. Chances will come my way. We spend the rest of the game hitting them on the break and stuff them 3–1; 4–1 on aggregate.

Who needs away goals when you've scored four?

*****

Then along come Barcelona in the final.

The greatest club team in the world.

The game is being held in the Stadio Olimpico in Rome, with its long walk from the dressing room to the pitch and its firecrackers and flares. The home support – Roma and Lazio share the ground – aren't here tonight, but the place is still edgy, buzzy. Everyone's fired up, fans and players.

Before the game The Manager sets us up with five men in midfield – including me – with Ronaldo up top. 'The aim is to hit them on the counter-attack,' he says before the game. 'We try to contain them and not get overloaded in midfield. If we can break their play up and hit back, we will pinch a goal.'

We start well. Our midfield presses them high up the pitch, but they're a team of masters, especially the midfielders Xavi and Iniesta; their tiny striker, Lionel Messi, is arguably the only player stopping Ronaldo from being talked up as the best footballer on the planet and is a forward who can do the maddest things with a football. I watch him on the Spanish football shows on the telly and in the Champions League games all the time, so I know how good he can be. The goals he puts away are incredible because he makes everything look so easy. He scores goals by beating players

– three, four, five defenders, he walks round the lot of them. He scores goals from headers and free-kicks as if it's no big deal. He gets battered by defenders quite a lot as well, but he always gets up. He doesn't moan or roll around holding his face. He dusts himself down and scores more goals.

With Messi leading the line, pulling us apart, gaps open up in our defence and Barcelona get in behind our midfield. We can't get a grip on the game; I can't even get the ball off them. Those three players are so skilful, so quick that we can only chase shadows as they pass the ball and move around the park.

We start off really well for the first few minutes. Their defender, Gerard Pique, has to make a great block to stop us from scoring, but then they take charge of the game, passing the ball around us like we're not even there.

Pass.

Move.

Pass. Move.

Passmovepassmovepassmove.

They're quick and dead small, all of them. The minute I put my arm up in a challenge, it's face high, so the ref gives a free-kick every time.

Pass.

Move.

Pass. Move.

Passmovepassmovepassmove.

They score early through Samuel Eto'o after 10 minutes and spend the rest of the game playing keep ball, like it's a laugh, a park game. It's so frustrating because we can't get into the match. It's tiring, too. We're chasing shadows, tracking players, putting in challenges without getting a grip on the contest. We don't get the ball in the areas we want. When we do get the ball we're so knackered we give it back. Then they break us down and score a second – this time it's a header from Messi. They win 2–0. I hate watching them lift the trophy afterwards.

Later that night, we have a party, as we always do at the end of a season: wives, girlfriends, the coaching staff, everyone's there, but for the first couple of hours it's horrible. Moody. No one's really speaking.

After a bevvy I try to cheer up some of the lads: 'Come on, don't be soft, we have to move on. There's a Premier League trophy sitting over there, it's ours.'

The atmosphere starts to lift a little. One by one people start getting photos with the cup. It takes time, but the party soon gets underway. For most of the evening everyone's putting on a brave face because losing the Champions League final is a choker, but at least we still have a Premier League trophy to our name at the end of a hard season.

The best trophy.

Fact.

CHAPTER
16
NIGHTMARE

9 July 2009.

The first day back at pre-season training.

I'm like most blokes, I put on a few pounds after a holiday. Even if I don't train for a week, I put on two or three, but when I get back to Carrington for the first day of work, I'm in for a shock. The scales in the club gym tell me I've put on a few more pounds than expected.

Seven.

Seven!

Then I remember: I drank a few bevvies while I was away. I'm stocky; I'm not like Ryan Giggs, all bone and lean muscle, I gain weight quite easily. It's not a problem though. It's not as if The Manager's leaning over my shoulder as the numbers come in, tutting and making jokes about me eating too many chip butties. Besides, I know I can shift it in a week or two.

All the players are given loose training programmes to stick to while they're away, but they're optional. The club like us not to go overboard on the eating and drinking in the close season break (but they're usually OK if I go a bit overweight), so if I go abroad I like to get into the hotel gym three times a week to work on the treadmill and do some weight work. That way I can be sharp when we get back to training and the running will feel easier when the pre-season games start.

When it comes to nutrition, all the players know what to eat and what not to eat all year round, but we allow ourselves some luxuries. During the season, I don't think there's any harm having a takeaway every now and then. The club always has someone on hand to talk to me about diet if I need them. Their big thing is that they don't like me to drink too much caffeine – I usually have a hit before a game and it won't have the effect I'd like if I've been knocking back coffee all week. An energy drink before every match always gives me a boost, but it's probably more mental than physical.

Coming back for pre-season after a few bevvies and a few weeks away from a ball is physically tough, not that anyone would have guessed by the mood in the dressing room as the lads get together for the first time. Everyone's excited to be in work again. The jokes are flying around and everyone looks dead healthy, tanned. It feels like the first day back in class after the school holidays. We've all got stories to tell, people are talking about their breaks away and everyone's laughing. *Footballers are big kids at heart.*

There are new players to say hello to as well. Antonio Valencia and Michael Owen have arrived following their summer transfers to United. For Michael it's easy meeting the team as he knows pretty much everyone here, either because he's played against them in the Premier League or with them for England; Valencia has come from Wigan Athletic and is saying hello to a lot of the lads for the first time. Everyone's trying to make him feel at home, letting on to him, having a crack.

Most of all, I'm looking forward to seeing him play and sussing out what he's made of. I can tell a lot about a footballer by the way he is in the dressing room and by the way he works at Carrington. I'm always excited when a new lad comes to the club, especially if they're a forward or an attack-minded player. I want to know how they operate; I'm looking to build a partnership with them on the practice ground. If they're keen to graft in training and put the effort in, then I know they'll fit in to the club.

The other changes today are that Carlos and Ronaldo have gone. Ronnie's move wasn't a shock really. Real Madrid came in for him; he's a *Galactico* now. I think we'd all had a feeling that he was set to leave in the summer because he'd been brilliant all year for us and the papers were constantly speculating that he was going to Madrid. Ronnie had wanted to go there, it was an ambition for him, plus he was always moaning about the Manchester weather.

'It's too cold here!' he'd complain in February when the rain was chucking down. Then again everyone moans about it – the foreign lads, even the English players.

I remember at one point last season, the speculation about Ronnie and Madrid got so bad that when it came to practice matches in training we'd always put him in a white bib, just so we could wind him up about it.

'Look at you!' we'd shout. 'You're already in the kit!'

It was hardly a shock when I picked up the paper by the pool on holiday and saw the news that he was off. It's a shame though. He's a nice lad and an amazing footballer. We'll miss him.

Carlos's move wasn't a surprise, either, but the fact that he's gone to Manchester City (of all places) is. It's a loss for the team, but it's probably good news for Patrice. Carlos never bothered to learn the lingo in the end and Patrice was constantly explaining to him what was being said in club meetings and team talks.

I liked Carlos when he was at the club; we got on because we both had the same work ethic on the pitch. He had bags of energy and he did a lot of work whenever he played. He ran so hard in games that some days at Carrington he couldn't do the training; he was wrecked from the weekend's work. It never had an impact on his game though. He was always class when it came to match day.

I felt a bit bad for Carlos because he couldn't seem to get into The Manager's starting XI. He hadn't done a lot wrong, but myself, Ronaldo and Berba were playing so well that he found himself sitting on the bench most games. He became disappointed, which is the natural reaction for a footballer, I suppose. Towards the back end of the season we all knew he was more likely to leave than not because players like Carlos always want to start matches. Still, I'm a bit surprised he's signed for City.

Someone mentions a billboard that's been put up in the centre of town.

'It's a massive, sky blue poster with Carlos on it. It says "Welcome To Manchester,"' says one of the lads.

No one really seems that arsed. Most of the time, publicity stunts like that go over the players' heads, but I can understand if the fans are a bit annoyed by it. United and City dominate Manchester. I reckon our lot will feel annoyed at seeing Carlos in a sky blue shirt. They might think that the poster is nothing more than a cheap shot, but there's that many advertising boards around town that I haven't even seen it. I've only really heard about it in the papers and from the lads today.

I'm mainly thinking about how it's going to be an uncertain time for United and the club. *How are we going to replace those two world-class players?* Then The Manager comes down to the dressing room to have a word. The mood soon changes. Everyone goes quiet.

He welcomes us back; he tells us how well we played to win the league in May. He tells us we'll have to play even better to win it again this year because of the strength of Chelsea, Arsenal and Liverpool, but also because of City and their money.

'But believe in yourselves, lads,' he goes. 'Because we still have plenty of talent to win the league, even though we've lost two great strikers.'

Then he lets on to me. He tells me he wants me to score more goals, especially with Ronaldo and Carlos gone.

'I want you to get in the box and get on the end of more chances, Wayne.'

'But boss, I've been playing out wide. Do I have to get on the end of my own crosses now?'

I'm being cheeky, but I know what he means.

'There are going to be games where I'm going to have to play you upfront on your own, Wayne,' he says, which leaves me feeling dead chuffed. It's what I was hoping for because now I can concentrate on scoring goals and influencing the game how I like. No more running up and down the wing for me, chasing overlapping full-backs about.

Then we go to work.

Time for our exams.

At the end of the 2008/09 season, all the players took tests measuring our body fat and heart rate. My first task in pre-season is to have them taken again and it's murder: blood tests, coaches measuring the muscular stretches of every player in the squad; everyone does a treadmill test. I'm given an oxygen mask and for 18 minutes I have to run at a set pace. On every third minute a doctor draws blood. From various checks he measures my fitness levels and general health. Throughout the season, United's fitness coaches and doctors constantly look back at the results so they can assess my levels of strength, stamina and physical health. The doc tells me he could suss if I had a cold coming just by taking a few tests and comparing the results to my summer paperwork.

When the medicals are done and everyone has finished their lunch in the canteen, I drive home with one thought in my head: *I'll be playing up front all season.*

I'm made up, especially after playing so many games on the wing over the last couple of years. It's going to be an exciting campaign. If there's one downer to the day it's that I know tomorrow will be a lot tougher at Carrington.

I'm going to pay for that holiday.

*****

The next morning the footballs come out and everything we do involves running with the ball – sprinting, jogging, five-a-sides, all of us are getting used to having a footy at our feet again after the long break. Not all clubs are the same, though. At Everton, I don't remember seeing a football until the second week of pre-season and the coaches used to make us run until we couldn't move another step.

Today, the longest run we do lasts 45 seconds. It's carried out at a high intensity; it's not the hardest burst of physical exercise I'll ever do in my life, but then the drills get harder. The Manager wants us to do a double training session – morning and afternoon work. We have an Asian tour coming up and he wants us to be fit for it. The pitches get longer, the full-size goals come out. Suddenly I'm going for those long sprints, the ones I'll have to make during every match in the Premier League. My lungs burn; I move up and down the park non-stop.

We play a 90-minute game and my heart's banging. Everyone's battered after an hour. The following day, we play again. It takes 75 minutes for the pain to kick in. A week later the whole team are still strong at full-time. That's how United like us to be. It's important that we maintain our high levels of fitness because we've had so much success in the past by pressing and attacking until the final whistle. We've always pushed to score, whether we've been winning, losing, or on level terms. We've never lumped hopeful balls into the box, hoping to get lucky. We've always played passes out wide and fired crosses into dangerous areas. To do that, we've had to be dead fit.

Now we are.

A couple of days later we go on tour to Asia: Malaysia, South Korea and China. We fly 16 hours to Malaysia and play a Malaysian XI in the Bukit Jalil Stadium, Kuala Lumpur. We fly to South Korea and play FC Seoul in the World Cup Stadium. And then we fly to China and play Hangzhou Greentown FC in the Yellow Dragon Stadium. Then we fly home.

The trip last 10 days. It takes a lot out of the players with the jet lag and the travelling, but the support when we're there is incredible. The stadiums are packed with 70,000 people whenever we play; there are hundreds of fans taking pictures wherever we go. I can't leave my hotel because it's like Beatlemania outside, but The Manager still gives the lads a night off, so we all go out for a meal. The whole team sits down for tea in a fancy restaurant, but before the menus have even come out, camera phones point at us from all angles.

*****

When the season starts a couple of weeks after the Asia tour, we start with a win against Birmingham (I get a goal) and a loss to Burnley away. Then I score in the next four games:

22 August, Wigan 0 Manchester United 5

29 August, Manchester United 2 Arsenal 1

12 September, Spurs 1 Manchester United 3

20 September, Manchester United 4 City 3

I love playing upfront on my own. Most of the time, I'm the focal point of the attack in a 4–5–1 formation and I buzz off it. I'm not involved in the game as much as I could be because I don't have to drop deep and defend anymore, but this means I'm conserving my energy until the very end of the game. My focus is on being in the right place at the right time, taking my chances and scoring goals.

The City game is the maddest result because Michael Owen scores the winner in the sixth minute of injury time and everyone goes nuts, most of all the City lot because they think we've had extra-time handed to us. 'Fergie Time' the papers call it; people start making out that The Manager is intimidating officials into giving us more minutes on the clock at the end of games when we need to score a goal.

How stupid is that? As far as I can tell, both teams were drawing and City had the same amount of stoppage time as us. I can't see what the problem is. If City are an ambitious team, as they keep saying they are, then they should be making the most of those seven minutes. They should be thinking: 'We've got time to get a goal.'

They didn't and we did; we knew that if we made chances, someone like myself or Michael would score a winner. That's one of the reasons why he was brought into the squad in the first place, to help me upfront whenever we switch to 4–4–2. He can make the difference in big games.

I get 13 goals by Christmas and one of the reasons for my improved goal rate is Antonio Valencia. He's a quick winger – good with his feet and a great passer of the ball. Ever since joining, he's been on fire. The crosses have flown into the box thick and fast in games and I've managed to get on the end of a lot of them, mainly because I've learnt in training that I have to be on my toes with him, probably more than I ever did with Ronaldo. Ronnie was sharp, but this fella moves in on the byline and crosses more quickly. His first instinct is to play the pass and that makes it easier for me to know when to burst into the box, or to get across my defender. I score against Blackburn, Pompey, West Ham and Wolves, and the team sits in second place behind Chelsea. I've got loads of confidence. Everything I try on the pitch seems to work. If I keep this up, 2009/10 could be my best season so far.

Maybe I can beat Ronnie's 42 goals from the other year ...

*****

I mess up.

Against Hull in the KC Stadium at the end of December, I score the opening goal in stoppage time at the end of the first half, an easy tap-in that lands on my plate after the Hull defence fails to sort out a Darren Fletcher cross. During the opening minutes of the second half we keep the ball and stay defensively tight. The plan is to score a second goal on the break, but then I make the type of mistake that gives every player 'mares: I underhit a back pass to our keeper, Tomasz Kuszczak.

I'm on the halfway line, under pressure and I decide to play the ball home so we can start again and build another attack, but I can tell from the moment I lay off the pass that I've underhit it – it's not going to reach the penalty area. Their striker, Craig Fagan nips in to thieve my soft pass and he's through on goal.

No! Where did he come from?

If it had happened at the other end, the fans would have been calling it a near-perfect through ball because it's perfectly weighted. Instead it's a prezzie that leaves Fagan with a one-on-one in our area. From that moment, I'm glued to the spot, like in one of those dreams where there's a chase but I can't leg it because my feet are dead heavy, like they're stuck in thick mud. It's horrible.

Fagan takes the ball past Kuszczak.

Please spoon it, please spoon it.

I feel helpless. I stand and watch as the game goes on around me. Everyone's watching me in the ground and on the telly. I feel like a divvy. I'm on my own with millions of people staring at my mistake. There are United fans swearing at me from their front rooms at home, most probably.

Please spoon it, please spoon it.

Fagan takes the ball too far; he floats a cross over Kuszczak. As Hull's Jozy Altidore comes over to nod the ball in, our full-back, Rafael Da Silva, bundles him over and the ref blows his whistle.

Penalty. *My fault.*

They score. *My fault.*

1–1. *My fault.*

A TV camera points at me and I look directly into the front rooms of everyone watching on the box. My face says it all: I'm terrified of losing and terrified of what The Manager will say to me about cocking up. Nobody in football would swap boots with me at this moment.

Then I hear that dreaded sound: The Manager shouting at me. My position on the halfway line means I'm close to the dugout. He's off the bench, yelling. I can't quite make out what he's shouting, but I know it isn't anything complimentary. I'm not going to turn around to get a better idea of what he's saying though; I don't want to get The Hairdryer.

I know the only way I can avoid a rollicking is if United win and I play out of my skin for the next half an hour. Luckily, both of these things happen. We win 3–1 and I set up the next two goals. I play so well that the people on Sky telly even give me the Man of the Match award afterwards.

When I get back to the dressing room, The Manager shakes the players' hands. Then he lets on to me.

'You were lucky,' he says and walks off.

I take a deep breath. I know then that if we'd lost or drawn against Hull, I'd have taken the blame.

*****

PREMIER LEAGUE TABLE, 9 JANUARY 2010

	PLAYED	GD	POINTS
1/ CHELSEA	20	29	45
2/ UNITED	21	27	44
3/ ARSENAL	20	30	42

*****

After Christmas we batter Wigan by five, draw with Birmingham and then win against Burnley, Hull (again; I score all four in a 4–0 victory), Arsenal and Pompey. We share honours at Villa. By mid-February we're still in second place. Then I get The Hairdryer again after a 3–1 defeat to Everton at Goodison later in the month.

It's no surprise because I play crap; it's one of my worst games ever and I give the ball away, miss chances and fluff passes. The ball keeps bouncing off me. There's nothing I can do to correct my mistakes and I feel terrible.

I can always tell in the early stages of a game if I'm off colour. My touch doesn't feel right almost immediately. The passes go wrong and the ball seems difficult to control, as if my footy boots are shaped like 50p pieces. I try a difficult pass, it doesn't go my way and I get frustrated. I try to make a tackle to settle my game down, but instead I kick the player. Eventually when I do get a chance in front of goal, I send it wide.

It's always important in games like this to fix the problem quickly. I go back to basics and make a few simple passes. I try to play the game calmly because I don't want to make any silly mistakes. After a few minutes of doing this, my confidence usually comes back.

Not today though. We go a goal up but Everton strike back within minutes. I can't really get a grip on this game. My touch is all wrong and I can feel a mood coming on. I try harder and harder, but it makes all the bad touches and misplaced balls that much more frustrating. I can't get past their defence. I can't *imagine* getting past their defence. They've become a mental block: they're bigger, faster, stronger than me.

I know low confidence is an enemy. I know it's all in my head, but there's nothing I can do. It's killing my normal game. Everything seems that much harder today and it's one of the worst feelings I know in football. By half-time I feel exposed, like I'm a goldfish in a bowl. It feels as if everyone's staring at me, but I can't perform. It's a bit like that nightmare again: I'm stuck in the mud and I can't run.

Then it gets worse because the Everton fans suss that I'm having a bad day. Every time I give the ball away they let out a sarky cheer.

The second half doesn't get much better.

When I'm playing like this, one of two things happen to me. The first is that I don't want the ball as much as normal because I worry I might give it away. I don't want to get involved in the game. I don't want to make a mistake. Thankfully, that happens so rarely, and it definitely won't happen today, not in front of the Everton lot.

Playing against Lionel Messi in the 2009 Champions League final. An amazing player. The things he can do with a ball are unbelievable.

Winning the Carling Cup in 2010. At United we take every trophy dead seriously.

The agony of my busted foot in the first leg of the 2010 Champions League semi-final against Bayern Munich.

Lining up in the tunnel against Bayern Munich for the second leg. It's long and dark, narrow and cramped. Psychologically, a lot of games are won here. We beat Bayern 3-2 on the night, but go out on away goals.

Leaving the hospital in my
cop boot after my ankle injury.
ring that thing drove me mad.

Winning the PFA Players' Player of the Year in 2010.
Personal accolades are nice but they mean nothing if
United don't get a trophy or two.

When The Manager's in a good mood (when
we're winning) he jokes with the players . . .

. . . but if I'm not playing to his high standards
then I often get The Hairdryer.

My overhead kick against City in 2011. Nani's cross got a deflection, which gave me the time to think, 'I'm having a go at this . . .'

I made a good connection with the pass and twisted in mid air to see the ball bobbing and spinning behind Joe Hart in their net . . .

Standing there with my arms spread wide, I could feel the hate coming off the City fans Old Trafford went mental.

Losing it at the cameras after my hat-trick against West Ham. The pressure was pouring out of me, like steam from a kettle. Time to say sorry. Another lesson learnt.

Scoring against Barca in the 2011 Champions League final at Wembley.
But it wasn't enough. We lost 3-1.

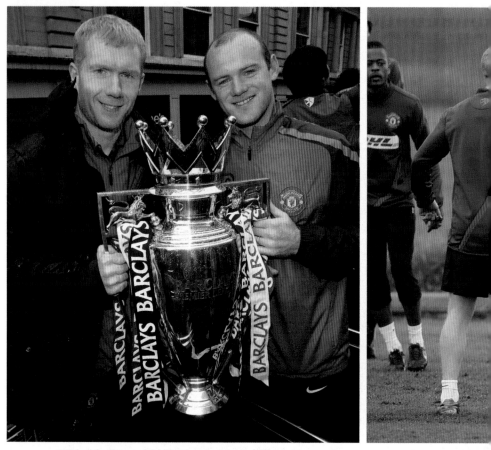

With Scholesy, probably the greatest midfielder to play in the Premier League.

A decade in football; the number 10 shirt. The hunger to win and score goals drives me on every day.

A keep-ball session at Carrington. Notice Patrice Evra's not wearing his shinnies; he must have thought Scholesy wasn't playing that day!

Scholesy snaps at Rio's ankles. I look happy that, for once, it isn't me on the receiving end.

Applauding the United fans. I'm grateful for all the support they've given me over the years, even through the bad times. *There are more good times to come.*

The other thing that can happen is that I work too hard. I try to force myself back into the action; I drop deep to win the ball back, but the deeper I drop into my own half, the harder it is for me to score. It also means that if I mess up, I can give the ball away in a dangerous area.

There have been games when I've run all over the park in this mood. When I've tried to change a game on my own: I've cleared the ball off the United goal line, I've closed down attackers in our penalty area. Then I've often been too tired for the closing stages of the game. When Everton score another two goals, that's exactly what happens: I start running all over the pitch, trying to regain possession.

Sometimes The Manager sees me having a bad day and tries to calm me down. Other times, he subs me.

I hate getting subbed. When I see a fourth official holding up the board with the Number 10 on it, I usually feel annoyed. I get fed up with myself. If I've not played well, I always know it, but I want to stay on to make up for the mistakes I've made.

But I'll admit it: there have been times when I've felt relieved to come off. If I've been having a 'mare and I've noticed the fourth official punching numbers into his board, I've sometimes thought, *Why don't you get me off? It's not going to happen today.*

Then once I'm sitting on the bench, I stew.

People say I often look moody when I've come off the pitch. Well, that's because I am moody, but that anger's not directed at The Manager, because I usually understand why he's made the decision. I look moody because I'm frustrated with myself. I take pride in my game. If I don't play well, I get upset.

Today The Manager keeps me on till the end and we lose 3–1.

In the dressing room afterwards, he yells at me.

'I'm never playing you at this stadium again! You can play so badly here!'

He might have a point. I often have a 'mare at Goodison because playing here is still a massive deal for me. I still want to show the Everton fans why I left them behind and what sort of player I've become. I still want to prove a point whenever I play here. Sure, I've played well in one or two games at Goodison, but I've also played really badly in others.

Today was the worst.

*****

When I get home after the Everton game, something strange happens. Coleen opens the door with our newborn son, Kai, in her arms. She smiles and says, 'Unlucky, Wayne,' then she hands me the baby. I walk indoors and look down at him in my arms. He looks up at me and smiles. *How can I be grumpy now?*

I smile back. I can't help but be happy because I want to play with him. He's only four months old but he's taking me out of my bad mood.

'Here, Coleen, we've lost the game and this is the first time I'm not stewing in it.'

She laughs. It's a first, we know. I used to take a black mood home with me whenever we'd got beat. After a defeat, I'd be grumpy all night; I'd be grumpy the next day, too. I used to sit on the couch sulking and I wouldn't shift for hours. I'd watch the telly because I couldn't get to sleep until three or four in the morning. I'd be replaying the game in my head, reliving the mistakes over and over, wasting hours feeling sorry for myself.

It's funny, when I score great goals or do something dead smart on the football pitch, everything happens so quickly that I don't get to enjoy it for long. Afterwards, when I'm replaying everything back in my head like a DVD, I find it hard to see those split-second decisions. I can't remember the touch that brought a long pass down. I can't remember feeling the ball leaving my boot. I can't remember that instant where I've realised my shot has gone beyond the goalie's fingertips and into the back of the net.

When I make a mistake I remember everything.

It's crystal clear and in a freeze frame for days afterwards. I relive it all before I go to sleep. And when I think about it, I feel embarrassed. It's horrible.

Maybe fatherhood puts it all into perspective. I have a great passion for football and winning, but now that I have a family I have other responsibilities. At this moment, I have to give Kai my time; I have to be a dad. I can't be moody anymore. I have to deal with the nightmare games on my own.

Things have changed ...

*****

But not that much.

I can't help the way I am. Even though I'm in a better mood than normal after the Everton game I still hate losing more than anything. I know I haven't played well and when Kai's gone to bed, I have a right go at myself. After dinner I watch the game back; I analyse the things that I've done wrong. As I see the mistakes on the box I get really wound up, but I can only think of one thing: *I can't wait for the next match.*

I want to put Everton behind me by playing well in the next fixture against West Ham. Until the whistle goes again the bad performance is going to be on my mind. It's going to drive me on in training; it'll make me run harder all week. It'll even keep me awake at night.

I can't wait for the next match.

*****

We beat West Ham, 3–0; I score two. Talk about putting a bad game behind me.

CHAPTER
17
PASSION

I'm the same as any football fan in the country: when the fixtures are announced in the summer, I scan them quickly, picking out the most important matches.

I look for Everton first.

I look for Liverpool.

I look for City.

Then I look for Arsenal and Chelsea, the crunch games in the title race. I look at our opponents on the first and last day of the season; who we're playing in the Christmas break. But really, no league fixtures are as important to me as the games against Everton, Liverpool, City and whoever might stop us from winning the title.

Then I look for other matches that might affect me, like the Merseyside derby. I make a point of watching those games as a supporter if I can. I can't help it. I'm still an Everton fan and I still get really nervous whenever I watch them on the box. I get upset if they lose. I shout and swear at the telly, I moan at the ref if he gives a bad decision against them. I've even got Kai a tiny Everton kit. We dress him in it for the games when they're playing on the telly.

I'm not the only one though. Rio tells me that he always keeps an eye out for the West Ham results when they come in. Michael Carrick always wants Newcastle to win, except when they're playing us. We all understand what it's like to be sat in a packed stadium, watching a team we love, getting that buzz when they win and that sick feeling when they lose. That's why it's a massive thing to be loved by the supporters of the club I play for.

Whenever I turn out for United, the fans always sing the same thing:

'Rooney!'

'Rooney!'

'Rooooooo-neeeee!'

It starts in a little corner of the ground and it builds. It gets bigger and bigger until it's echoing around the whole stadium. As it happens I'm usually focusing on the game so I don't often hear it, but if play has stopped and I catch the sound of my name ringing around the ground, it helps to sharpen my concentration even more. I use it to push me on. Sometimes it gives me goose bumps.

'Rooney!'

'Rooney!'

'Rooooooo-neeeee!'

I hear it when I walk onto the pitch and it pumps me up. When I hear it after I've made a great tackle or I've scored, I can get a bit emotional. I feel my chest puffing up with pride. The crowd are on their feet, cheering, waving their flags, singing.

'Rooney!'

'Rooney!'

'Rooooooo-neeeee!'

It's an unbelievable feeling.

*****

Every game is a massive event at United, but some matches seem to take over the whole town. At Everton it was always the Merseyside derby. At Old Trafford it's the fixtures against Liverpool and Man City – Liverpool because of the great successes they've had over the years and City because they're our neighbours.

It's double trouble for both Manchester teams this year, because we draw City in the Carling Cup semi-final. Two games, home and away. Two more derbies. For a week before the first leg on 19 January at their place, the fans say the same thing to me whenever I see them.

We have to win. We can't not win.

While the supporters are going mad for the game, in training The Manager keeps us calm. He maintains our focus. He prepares us like it's any other fixture, he tells us to concentrate on our technique. He understands that if we play our usual game then we'll have a great chance of winning the match, because we're a much better side than City.

'If you keep your heads and play football, we'll beat them every time,' he tells us. 'If you lose your heads, it gives their lot a chance. The crowd can get behind them and form will fly out of the window. It doesn't matter if City are the best team in the league or the worst; if you lose your cool, they'll win the game.'

But when the time comes for us to prepare ourselves mentally – in the team meeting on the night before the match – he gets us as fired up as the punters in the stands. He tells us that it's not just the points that are at stake, it's local passion and local pride.

'It means everything to the people out there.'

The English players get it straightaway, they know. Michael Owen comes up to me after the meeting – he can't believe how psyched up The Manager is, how he's got the entire squad going. He says, 'Oh my god. That's one of the best things I've ever heard.'

Sometimes it's the foreign lads who need some advice, some winding up, because the atmosphere and importance is new to them. They have to be told about the size of the derby and the size of the event. The rivalry, the noise, the aggression. It's something they might not have experienced before, certainly not in a game as big as the Manchester derby. If a player isn't ready for it, the rush and intensity of the game can come as a shock.

They say, 'Oh, City were mid-table last season. This should be easy.'

I tell them it's not. I tell them it's never easy and that it means a lot to everyone involved in the club. They should be prepared, but sometimes the team talks and the warnings don't work, like the run up to our 2010 FA Cup Third Round game against Leeds United. The match takes place in the same month as the City game and The Manager pulls all the players together at training.

'This will be the toughest game of the season.'

I can see some of the foreign lads looking around. They seem confused.

'How is it going to be the most difficult game of the season?' says Nemanja Vidic. 'They're in League One.'

The Manager spells it out for him. He warns him about the rivalry between the two teams and the hatred the fans have for each other. He talks about the underdog spirit and the magic of the FA Cup. Vida seems to get it, but the next day we lose and get knocked out of the competition. Even the best-laid plans can fly out of the window sometimes.

*****

As the date arrives, I notice the mood changing in Manchester. More and more kits are being worn around town. Everyone's talking about it – in the supermarket, the pubs, on the street. United fans tell me to batter the other lot; City fans ask me to go easy.

It's different to the Merseyside derby, though. When I played for Everton, we were always the underdogs, everyone reckoned Liverpool would win. These days I experience the opposite: United win most of the Manchester derbies and the fans expect us to win, home and away. At Everton, a draw was a good result. At United a draw is a poor one.

On the night of the game, I can feel the atmosphere building in the ground. It's mad, the most hostile mood I can imagine. When we arrive at their place their fans boo me from the minute I get on to the grass for the warm up. They sing songs about me. They call me this, that and the other.

I love it.

I love it because it means I annoy them, I get under their skin. They're doing it because they're frightened I might hurt them, cause some damage, maybe grab a goal. They want to stop me from scoring against them and they'll do anything to put me off my game. It never bothers me. They can boo as much as they like. I want us to batter City tonight.

*****

Things don't go well. We outplay City for the best part of 90 minutes and take an early lead through Giggsy, but then they get a penalty and Carlos steps up to take it. I try my best to wind him up. Even though he's a pal of mine, even though he used to give me a lift to the airport whenever we played Champions League games, I want him to blow it. I jog up to him and lean down as he places the ball on the spot.

I whisper, 'Don't hit the post, Carlos. Whatever you do, don't hit the post.'

He doesn't. He tucks it away and sprints towards the United bench to make gestures at Gary Neville. Apparently Gary had taken a pop at Carlos in the press after he'd left the club for City; when Carlos runs over to the touchline to gesture to Gaz on the bench, Gaz reacts and gives it back because he hates City.

I later ask Gary what happened and he tells me that he'd said in the papers that if The Manager had chosen not to sign Carlos permanently, then it was the right decision because The Manager hadn't made many bad decisions during his time at the club. Carlos had obviously seen it on the morning of the game and was taking it the wrong way. It doesn't help the bad mood in the stadium when he later scores a winner and starts gesturing to Gary again.

By the time the second leg comes around we're really up for it. City are talking a lot before the game about their plans and ambitions. They're looking to qualify for the Champions League, especially after spending a lot of money in the summer. We know we have to put them in their place.

We know we have to win.

We get off to a good start and lead 2–0. It puts us 3–2 in front on aggregate. Then, suddenly, Carlos scores again to bring the game level. With the match looking like it's going into extra-time, I get my head onto a cross. It loops up over Shay Given, drops into the back of the net and Old Trafford goes mental.

One half of the city goes mental.

We're going to Wembley again!

I love scoring in a derby game because it's extra special. It means something to the club and it means so much to the fans. It gives them something to lift their mood for the rest of the week. I feel like I've put one over on the other lot for them, maybe scooped them a few quid in bets. It's even better getting a winner in the last minute because there's no coming back from it.

That night I drive home and watch the goal over and over again on the telly. I'm buzzing so much I can't sleep. I have a glass of red wine to relax; I turn on the Xbox and play a football game to tire myself out, logging into an online game under my own name.

I play a United fan. He's talking to me through the head-set that links the two players over the internet. He has no idea he's playing the real Wayne Rooney and figures I'm just another United supporter using the name for a laugh. He starts chatting about the City game.

'Did you see Rooney's winning goal tonight?' he says. 'It was brilliant.'

I laugh. I know the excitement of getting the winner is going to live with me for weeks but I don't let on to him who I am. Instead I sit there, making passes with the game pad, a massive grin plastered across my face.

No mate, I didn't watch the game.

'It was great,' he says. 'Last-minute winner.'

Once we finish playing, I put the game on again. I watch it over and over. I'm awake for hours afterwards. Like every United fan in the country, I can't wait to go to work tomorrow.

*****

I've scored 26 for the season.

It's only February. I can still match Ronaldo's 42 goals. Then, in the knockout stages of the Champions League – the last 16 – against Milan in the San Siro, we win 3–2 (I score twice) and the home crowd whistle and boo every time I get the ball. Can't blame them really. I've scored six in six games against Milan, and I feel like I'm in the form of my life. It gets even better when I grab the winner against Villa in the Carling Cup final at Wembley a couple of weeks later.

I start on the bench; The Manager plays Michael Owen up top. Even though I'm not on the pitch, I'm thinking about being out there, firing one past the keeper. As a sub, I'm always watching the game closely. I think it's why I always do well when I come on if ever I've been rested.

I sit there at Wembley, not moody because I've been dropped, but looking, watching the play, taking the whole game in, dying to get on. James Milner scores an early pen for them, Michael equalises for us shortly afterwards, but rather than watching the game as a fan would, I'm working out exactly where the space is opening up on the pitch. I'm looking at which Villa players are tiring on their feet. They're the ones I'm going to attack if I get on.

Then Michael gets injured after half an hour, and I'm ready as soon as The Manager gives me the nod to get warmed up, but even though I'm alive from the minute my number goes up on the fourth official's board, the first few runs on the park feel like hard work. I remember Ryan Giggs telling some of the younger players in the squad – Jonny Evans, Danny Simpson – that it doesn't matter how much you warm up on the sidelines, you're always knackered for that first run on the pitch. He's right. It must be the adrenaline that does it. I'm dead fit but breathing hard as I leg it after the first through ball.

There's a lot of running to be done because it's a quick game and one of those matches that neutral fans love: wide open, 100 mph football where a goal could come at either end. Martin O'Neill is the Villa boss and he likes his team to soak up the pressure and attack on the break; we're dominating possession but struggling to crack their midfield. Villa are so quick up front it's frightening, especially with winger Ashley Young and striker Gabriel Agbonlahor. One mistake from us could lead to a goal. Our fans are edgy.

By the time the second half gets under way, I feel sharp. It's mad, for a couple of months now, every game I play, I know I'm going to score, and this one is no different.

A chance is coming my way. And I'm going to take it when it does.

I suppose that's the self-belief and focus all strikers need if they're going to score lots of goals at the top level. Sure enough, the chance I hoped for comes when Antonio Valencia breaks on the right-hand side of Villa's box.

He lays it off to Berbatov in the penalty area.

Berba backheels a return pass through the Villa defence and Valencia gets onto it fast.

He checks. I gamble, pushing onto the penalty spot. I know roughly where his pass is heading because I've seen this move a lot in training recently.

A seven-a-side at Carrington.
Berba collecting the ball, holding it up in the area.
Other players in training bibs moving into space.
A smart pass to a teammate – Nani, Valencia, Ji-Sung Park, or Ryan Giggs – then a ball across the box.
Pass. Move. Goal.

The attack depends on Berba. One of his strengths is bringing other players into the game, whether it's at Carrington, Old Trafford or Wembley. His touch is fantastic; he can bring an 80-yard clearance down with his boot like it's a pillow. Some fans reckon he's lazy because his body language is quite relaxed, but to me he's one of the most unselfish players I've ever played with. He doesn't mind not scoring as long as United win. And he's great at unlocking tight defences like the one Villa have today.

The mad trick here is the understanding between my teammates. Berba has the ball, so Valencia knows to leg it for the cute through pass. Once Valencia picks up his lay-off, I know I have to time my run into the box from his movement. As soon as he's two steps away from the ball, I pull away from my marker.

Right now, the hard part is choosing exactly where to run. This is always a guess. I haven't seen the ball leave Valencia's toes yet, so the cross could be heading towards the near post or somewhere behind me. I'm relying on luck, but today I play it just right: I move towards the penalty spot and now the ball is coming right for me. In a split second I have to decide what to do next.

Do I turn my marker?

Should I bring the ball down and shoot, or attack with my head?

But there's really no time to work it out. I'm in position. I'm set. The pass is on me. I see the ball, the goal, a defender's elbow as he comes to intercept …

I'm going to get smashed.

I glance the ball up and over the keeper.

Goal!

A header!

2–1!

That's how quickly it happens, the winning goal. It's the one I dreamt of scoring when I woke up this morning. It's the goal I dreamt of scoring as a kid – I've always fantasised about scoring the winning goal in a tight final at Wembley, but right now I'm not 100% sure how I've actually done it. I'm still not sure until I see the action replay on the box later that night, because it's so instinctive.

I can practise for hours, five days a week in front of goal, hitting shot after shot, or working on heading drills. And while these routines improve my game and build muscle memory, my instincts can't be coached. In that split second, I'm basically reacting to the target, which was the top right corner of the goal. The decision to head, shoot, bring the ball down, or turn my marker is a snap thought that happened without thinking. It's one in probably a million decisions that I don't even know I'm making during a game.

I'm not the only one either. No footballer at any level really has the time to analyse how they're going to react. That's a luxury nobody gets. Well, I don't. James Collins, the

Villa centre-half who marked the space on the penalty spot at Wembley moments earlier, didn't get it either. In height, Collins has inches on me. He's also built like a tree. I just got there first. I reacted quicker. And that's the difference between winning and losing, success and failure.

CHAPTER

18
PAIN

Playing footy in the Premier League is like having an addiction – it's taken over my life. It's the first thing I think about when I wake up in the morning, it's the last thing I think about before falling asleep at night. I even fantasise about it: I always daydream about winning big for Manchester United. It's what inspires me because playing for United is a huge high. The size of the club and the expectations of the fans mean that everything is magnified. The crowds are big, the expectations are big, and the goals give me a massive buzz.

Most of the time, kicking a footy around is all that I want to do. Whenever I wander around our house, walking from room to room, I've got one at my feet. Whenever I'm talking on the phone, I'm sitting back in my chair, doing small keepy-ups on my toes. And like any obsession, when I can't play, I get down. I get fed up. I remember one of the lads comparing playing football to alcohol one day. 'Playing for me is like beer is for most people,' he said. 'What's somebody going to be like if they can't have a beer for eight months? They're not going to be able to wait until they get to the pub for the first time and have a beer. And that beer's going to taste great.'

I can see what he means. I'm a footy obsessive: when I can't play with the ball, I hate it. It's so bad that whenever I get injured in a game, like I do against Bayern Munich in the 2009/10 Champions League quarter-final, the first thing I think about is the next fixture and whether I'm going to be fit enough to play.

When I'm laying face down in the turf at Bayern's Allianz Arena, one hand clutching my busted foot, the other waving to the bench for help, the season's fixtures race through my mind.

Will I be fit for the Chelsea game on Saturday? Ninety minutes are on the clock, the game is in the balance at 1–1. I'm in agony, but I can't help myself.

Is the season over?

Then it gets worse: as I lay there, Bayern score a winner. I can tell because of the deep, moody roar that rocks around the stadium like it does whenever a big German team gets a goal. I'd given us the lead after 64 seconds to go one-up; now we're 2–1 down. A good result turned bad.

Will I be OK?

Rob, the United physio rushes over. The final whistle goes. He checks my foot, squeezing the boot, feeling the ankle, checking for breaks. It kills so badly that I can't talk and I'm gutted because it was such a cheap injury to get. I was legging it back, chasing the ball when Bayern's striker, Mario Gomez, cut across me. I'd already picked up a yellow card so I checked my run, knowing any contact would send him flying. The ref would have given me a second card for sure, and that would have meant a suspension. It's funny what you can instinctively remember in a split-second, a heat of the moment challenge like that. Don't believe any player who reckons he's forgotten that he's on a yellow when he's playing footy. It's always on his mind.

The annoying thing is, if I'd tackled him, I wouldn't have got hurt. Instead, I jumped out of the way. My left foot landed and Gomez accidentally stood on it. His studs hit my toes. When my right foot landed, the ankle rolled over and my boot slipped awkwardly underneath, sending a shot through my foot.

I know it's bad from the second I trip because the pain is so severe. My ankle is in proper agony.

Rob helps me off the pitch.

'How long will I be out for?'

He thinks it might be ruptured ligaments.

'Can I play at the weekend?'

He pulls a face. 'Maybe four to six weeks out.'

I can't get my head around it. 'You're kidding?'

I'm gutted. It's the obsession. A month to six weeks means no Bayern Munich at home in the Champions League, no Chelsea, no Blackburn, no City, no Spurs, no Sunderland and no Stoke City in the league. Season over.

The final whistle goes. I can't face going off on a stretcher with everyone looking down on me from the stands, so Rob and the club kit man, Albert, help me from the pitch. I've got an arm around them both as I hobble off. Giggsy and the other lads gather round as we struggle down a flight of stairs that takes us away from the pitch. We're jostling with Bayern players, UEFA officials, cameramen and people in Champions League bibs in the cramped tunnel. Then we have to get up another flight of stairs to the dressing room. This isn't easy.

When I finally sit down, Rob puts my ankle in ice. I'm dead angry, I can't talk. All I can think about are the games I'm not going to be playing in, the training I'm going to miss.

The Manager asks me how I am.

'My foot's hanging off,' I tell him.

'Don't worry, it's going to be OK, Wayne,' he says.

But I'm not so sure it will be. Rob and the club doctor want to get me to the nearest hospital so I can get my ankle scanned, but they've been given more bad news: I've been selected for a random drugs test and there's no getting out of it, busted foot or no busted foot. The only way UEFA are going to let me off is if my injury is really dangerous – like a broken leg – or if I'm out cold.

'You've got to do it Wazza,' says Rob.

After 10 minutes of ice, he gently slides my foot into a protective boot. He hands me some crutches and takes me to the testing room. I want to get my foot scanned in the hospital; everyone wants to get my foot scanned, but instead I have to sit here with Patrice, two Bayern players and a couple of blokes from UEFA while we all wait to pee into some plastic containers.

It's always weird getting a drugs test and this is no different. First of all, I'm sitting in a room with two players from the opposition, which feels odd. Sometimes I know the lads who are there, other times I don't. Today, the two Bayern players are subs and I don't know who they are. We let on to them, they let on to us, but nobody really says anything. I sit in silence, wondering how long it'll be before I can pee. Probably ages. I've been playing football for 90 minutes. I'm completely dehydrated. It's the least of my worries though.

My season might be over.

We have drug tests all the time at United and they're never fun. Usually we get selected for testing by a lottery, though I remember a couple of days before the last game against City a team of FA testers came down to take samples from the England lads. Me, Rio, Michael Carrick – we all had to go.

Once I've been selected, the testers follow me from the minute I leave the training pitch to make sure I don't do anything dodgy with my sample. They watch me getting undressed, they watch me shower. They stand there looking at me until the second I finish peeing. Then they send my sample off with a whole load of paperwork to a test centre. The thing is, they never put my name on the form, just in case somebody in the centre doesn't like me and decides to do something to my sample. Three weeks later I get a letter giving me The All Clear.

At the Allianz Arena, I'm the last one out of the drug testing room because it takes me an hour to go to the loo.

*****

The worst thing about having an injury as a footballer is that everyone wants to talk about it, especially me.

Give me some good news, doc.

Rob reckons my ankle is so swollen with fluid and blood that there's no point having a scan tonight. When there's all that gunk floating around, a scan couldn't see any broken bones or ligament tears anyway. I'll have to wait until we land in Manchester the next day.

The team have gone back to the hotel after the Bayern game, so I ride back with the doctor in a private car. We drive past 50 photographers and they're all taking pictures of my crutches and the plastic boot. Another 50 photographers hang around for me at the airport in the morning. A car picks me up on the runway and whisks me through, but there's still time for them to take more pictures of my foot. In the afternoon, a mob waits for me at the hospital when I arrive – everyone wants to know if I'll be fit for the World Cup in South Africa in the summer. Afterwards, a film crew hangs around outside the gates of my house.

This is out of control.

The back page of *The Sun* that morning carries a photograph of me on the floor in the Allianz Arena. I'm holding my busted ankle. The headline reads: 'Pray'.

I can understand some of the hysteria because it's nearly the end of the season and the World Cup is only around the corner, but it still does my head in. I want to play as much as the fans want me to play. Thankfully, everyone gets their wish. By the time the doctor announces I've only burst some blood vessels and I should be fine in a couple of weeks, *The Sun* have written another headline.

'Wayne's Pain Is Only a Sprain So He's on the Plane.'

*****

It's crazy that doctors call the treatment for injuries like mine 'rehab'. That's where they usually send an addict for help, but then I'm a footy addict. After the Bayern Munich game I know I'll have to rest my ankle for a while; I can't train or help the lads prepare for the next match so, typically, I get grumpy, a bit like someone would when they have to give up smoking or coffee, I'd imagine.

I go to training a day or two later but can't kick a ball. I have breakfast with the team in the canteen and when it's time to start work, they go one way to the training pitches and I go the other to the physio's room and the gym. They're playing small-sided games. I'm having my ankle checked out. It's boring.

A lot of the rehab work I have to go through is pretty sci-fi. The doctor puts my ankle into an icing machine, then he lasers the damaged area. This quickens the recovery process by draining away the blood and fluid. The blood vessels are always moving around, the doctor tells me. He reckons that laser therapy speeds up this movement and helps the healing.

I'm a fidgety patient. I get snappy. I go quiet. I'm not fed up with the treatment or the physios and club doctors. I just want to get out there and play in the practice games like everyone else. I say sorry to Rob for my cob on.

'Don't worry pal, I'd rather you were moody about not playing than not bothered at all,' he says.

The worst thing is, rehab messes around with my head. I feel left out at the club. I miss the banter and the crack in the dressing room. As I'm not fit enough to play, I don't even get to spend the night in the team hotel with the rest of the lads before the next game against Chelsea. I have to stay at home and drive into the training ground the next morning for some more boring recovery work.

Still, it could be worse. Our midfielder, Owen Hargreaves, has had operations on both knees and hasn't played for 18 months. He was a regular for England and United before his injuries. He's missed out on so much, I don't know how he's got through it. A couple of days is bad enough for me; I reckon my head would go if I couldn't play football for a year and a half.

What's really strange, though, is that players become a spare part when they're seriously injured like Owen has been. They go off and do their own rehab work: Owen went to America; Anderson did his cruciate ligaments a couple of months back and I haven't seen much of him since. He's been doing a lot of his rehab in Portugal. The United physios stay in touch with the players when they're away, but they become forgotten men around the club for a while. When they come back to train with the lads again, it's like a little reunion.

I reckon The Manager leaves our recovery to the doctors because he has enough on his plate. He only needs to think about the players he can select for the team. The physios will tell him when someone like Owen or Anderson is ready to train properly again and from there he decides when to put them into the first team squad. He asks me how I'm feeling this week because there's a chance I might play against Bayern in the return leg, but we both know I haven't a hope of making Saturday's game against Chelsea at our place, which is a choker because it's one of our biggest fixtures of the season. It's between us and them for the league now; we're top and they're second, but if we lose they'll nick our spot and whoever wins will have a massive psychological advantage in the title race.

I wish I could play.

When the day comes I watch the game from a box in the stands. Before the start I get wound up and nervy. It's like being a fan all over again, just like the Barça game a couple of years back, and it's probably more nerve-wracking than actually playing. When the game starts it feels even worse than going to training and not being able to play, mainly because we lose 2–1, but also because it's so frustrating. I can't influence the game at all. I'm helpless. There's nothing I can do to change the result and help my mates win the match. I try to keep a happy face on when I'm around the other lads at Old Trafford afterwards, but it's hard. Chelsea have got the edge over us in the league, and it's a game we really needed to win.

Hopefully I won't have to wait long for my next game.

I wish I could play.

*****

'The news is good,' says Rob a couple of days later. 'You could be back for the home tie against Bayern Munich in a week.'

I'm made up. The Manager is pleased too, but he has a plan. He wants me to keep the protective boot on for a bit longer.

'Especially when you leave the training ground, Wayne,' he says. 'I want to give Bayern's scouts the impression that you're crocked for the return game.'

Sound. But the boot is a pain, and even though I can't feel a thing when I walk, it's still really clumsy and gets in the way of everything.

'This isn't stopping me from doing day-to-day stuff,' I tell Coleen, taking it off after I walk through the front door awkwardly. I'm determined about that, too. The next afternoon I run out of milk for Kai at home. Coleen is away for the day, so a mate drives me and the baby round to the garage to pick up some supplies. The guy behind the counter looks dead shocked when he sees me walking towards the counter on crutches, carrying a shopping basket full of semi-skimmed and a box of nappies for Kai.

*****

I get to take my boot off behind closed doors at training, but I can't yet run with the ball or put pressure on my ankle. It's important to keep my fitness up so when my injury heals I'll be match ready. Instead of playing, I go on a special treadmill the club has put into a small pool in the gym. The water supports me while I jog and cameras positioned in the bottom film the way my foot lands. It's tough work.

I do cardio work. I go on the bike and race through a set of gruelling sessions with a physio: 5000 metres, 2000 metres, 1000 metres, 500 metres and 200 metres. I pedal as fast as I can and my heart feels like it's going to burst at any second. Weirdly, it's the shorter sprints that are more knackering. Cycling 200 metres only takes 10 seconds but everyone who does it feels sick afterwards. Me and Darren Fletcher finish a bike session and afterwards we have to lay down in the dressing room because we both feel like throwing up. When I look in the mirror I'm as white as a sheet.

When I get to train properly again it's a relief, but some strange things go through my mind on the first day back with a ball. I'm full of mixed emotions. I wake up on the morning of my first session buzzing. I'm dead excited to be playing, but I'm also a little bit worried. I want to get through the session without any problems or twinges. I don't want to get hurt again, but I won't hold back in the sprints or tackles. I've got more chance of getting hurt if I hold back. I never let the possibility of an injury cross my mind when I'm on the pitch. I'll even take an injury for a goal. If it means getting hurt in order to get three points, I'll do it, and I'll play through pain, no problem.

Injuries don't affect the way I think about the game when I'm over the white line, but I can't imagine what it must have been like for players like Eduardo, Aaron Ramsey (both of Arsenal) and our former striker Alan Smith. All of them had really bad leg breaks and it must have made them a little bit worried when they came back for the first time after a knock like that. The confidence must go a bit.

I remember Alan's injury because it was horrible. It happened against Liverpool. He went to block a shot and landed awkwardly. The physio ran on and nobody really thought anything serious had happened because it looked like a minor incident. When I went over to the physio's bag for a bottle of water, I nearly chucked up: Alan's foot was facing in the opposite direction to his ankle. It was horrible.

The first thing I notice when I'm on the pitch if an injury like that happens is that the shock really changes the mood of the game. It shakes the players up. We were beaten by Liverpool that day, but immediately afterwards everyone was thinking about Alan. It could have been a career-threatening break. No one was talking about the game in the dressing room.

I get through the training sessions without a hitch – though my ankle still hurts – and by the time match day comes, I'm not even thinking about the pain, I'm thinking about getting us through to the Champions League semi-finals. I'm confident of scoring. I'm dead keen to play even though I'm not 100%: it's mad, in training I can sprint but I can't turn or stop suddenly. It's like my brakes have gone.

When my name is announced in the team line-up against Bayern, the Old Trafford crowd go mental. The ground is buzzing. It really gives us a lift and we come flying out of the traps. We go three-up in 41 minutes and the whole stadium starts singing my name:

'Rooney!'

'Rooney!'

'Roooo-neeeeee!'

It feels brilliant.

For a minute I reckon we could win by six or seven goals tonight, just like we did against Roma the other year. Then the whole thing comes crashing down as Bayern score twice. The pain gets too much – my ankle is throbbing. I hobble off the pitch again and watch from the sidelines as we go out on away goals. The Champions League is over for us.

I'm gutted. Everyone's gutted. When we head back to the dressing room, nobody talks. The Manager doesn't say anything. The whole team is in the same mindset: *We shouldn't have lost that game. It should have been us going through.*

It gets worse a few weeks later when I sit at home and watch Bayern batter Lyon in the first semi-final.

It should have been us.

Then Inter get past Barcelona in the other.

It should have been us.

'Football for me is like beer is for most people.'

Now I'll have to wait another season for my European fix.

*****

FINAL PREMIER LEAGUE TABLE, 2009/10

	PLAYED	GD	POINTS
1/ CHELSEA	38	71	86
2/ UNITED	38	58	85
3/ ARSENAL	38	42	75

One point.

One point.

Chelsea have too much for us in the end, but only just. Their victory at our place is enough to pinch the title. One point is enough to steal it. Fair play, neither of us were at our best this year; we both could have done better and we both slipped up a few times, but they had the edge on us. One of them things, I guess. It's just that after all those goals and all that promise we only won the Carling Cup.

And that feels like a bit of a let-down.

CHAPTER 19
CONTROVERSY

Then I let myself down.

I have a disastrous World Cup with England in the summer and I play badly. In the group stages I moan about the fans when they boo us off after a poor performance against Algeria. In the knockout phase we get battered 4–1 by Germany – it doesn't get any worse than that for an England player. The ankle injury that ends my season in 2010 gives me grief throughout the start of the 2010/11 campaign.

Unsurprisingly, my form takes a dive. I have 'mare after 'mare on the football pitch, I make silly mistakes and I rarely look like scoring. The only league goal I get comes in August against West Ham in a 3–0 win – a penalty. Then it gets worse. In September I'm dropped for the game against

Everton; my ankle puts me on the sidelines shortly after-wards. I get frustrated with myself, my game, my injury, and everything around me. I know I'm stuck in a cycle of bad form but I can't get out of it. And that's when I make the biggest mistake of my football career. In October, I release a statement which publicly questions my happiness at Old Trafford.

Am I better off elsewhere?

Everyone makes a fuss. There are discussions inside United to sort out the issue, people outside United chuck their opinions around, but the thing is, nobody really knows what's going on in my life. None of them understand where I am in my career; they don't know where my head's at. The only person who really knows what's going on in there is me, but even I'm not sure what I want.

Then The Manager has his say.

'Sometimes you look in a field and you see a cow and you think it's a better cow than the one you have in your own field. It's a fact, right? And it never really works that way.'

He's saying the grass isn't always greener, and he's right. Well, I don't see United as a cow, but the idea is right. *I like what's in my field. I'm wrong.* United want the same as me: trophies, success, to be the best. For six years, I've been lucky enough to win league titles and a Champions League trophy. I've been able to work alongside world-class players, not to mention The Manager, the most successful club boss in the modern game. My mind goes into another spin. I feel gutted at what I've done.

How stupid are you, Wayne?

What are you doing?

Then comes the moment of clarity.

You love the club, you love the supporters. You respect The Manager and he's got you trophies and titles. You couldn't be anywhere better. The club want the same as you: success, to be the best on the planet.

You'd be mad to leave. There's no better place to play than United. It's the biggest team in football. Our history is huge; you're playing with world-class players, and we're winners, sitting near the top of the table.

PREMIER LEAGUE TABLE, 30 OCTOBER 2010

	PLAYED	GD	POINTS
1/ Chelsea	10	24	25
2/ Arsenal	10	12	20
3/ United	10	10	20

That's when I make another decision, a sensible one this time.

Look, I want to stay.

I sign a new five-year contract with the club, but a strange atmosphere comes around the place. Some of the fans are moody about my announcement. When I run onto the pitch as a sub for the first time in weeks for the game against Wigan on 20 November, a lot of fans cheer me, but some of them boo. There are banners slagging me off. Fair play, I understand their opinions. The thing is, everyone makes mistakes. I just made mine in public, so I try to keep calm.

Get your head down, Wayne. Just get on with the game.

But the game doesn't come easy. I'm a bit short of match fitness because I've been on the sidelines for a few weeks and I don't start well. As the second half ticks away, I scuff a shot which I know would have gone a long way to getting me back on track.

I can feel it's a big miss, and by the time the final whistle goes, I'm gutted not to have kickstarted my season. But I have to keep going. I'm even more determined to prove to the fans that I'm the same player as before. *I'm having my worst season so far, but it's not like I'm about to hang my boots up.*

*****

I score a penalty against Rangers in the Champions League in the next game, but the league goals dry up. The fans are scratching their heads, trying to work out what's wrong with me. Some of them are wondering whether it's the end of an era, probably because when I do play well, the goals don't come and they don't see my name in the stats on the telly. Sure, a few chances go begging, but there are other times when goalies pull off world-class saves against me. On any normal day, a shot or two would have smashed into the back of the net. Instead they're getting pushed away, scrambled off the line, but it doesn't stop the negative talking.

In the pubs, on the radio, people are banging on about what I was as a player and how I've gone downhill. Experts and ex-footballers are writing all this rubbish about what I am and what I will be. They're chatting like the game's over for me. They've forgotten that a few months earlier I was voted the PFA Players' Player of the Year and The Football Writers' Association Footballer of the Year. Now, I'm being regarded as a no-mark. It's unbelievable how achievements are forgotten so quickly in football.

'He's past his best.'

'He's lost it.'

'He's not enjoying his football.'

'It's the beginning of the end.'

I try to shut it out. Every day for a couple of weeks, I think the same thing:

This bad run of form will pass, Wayne. You've got plenty of games and goals in you, it's just that you're on one of those dodgy spells that every footballer goes through from time to time. You haven't got to prove yourself to anybody. You just need to prove yourself to the fans. You just need to prove to them that your heart is still at Old Trafford, that you still want to play out of your skin for them.

For the next few months, make up for the mistake.

Convince them to forgive you.

Prove that you want the same thing as they do …

Glory.

*****

I miss a penalty against Arsenal; we still win 1–0.

Convince them to forgive you.

Three weeks later on New Year's Day I score in the 2–1 win over West Brom, my first goal in open play since March

2010. It's the beginning of a new year, but it feels like the beginning of a new season.

Convince them to forgive you.

A month later, I score two in a 3–1 win over Aston Villa.

Convince them to forgive you.

Then a couple of weeks after that, on 12 February 2011, I smash in the best goal of my career: an overhead kick against Manchester City that sends Old Trafford absolutely nuts and ends up being the winner in a 2–1 victory.

Prove that you want the same thing as they do.

I go nuts.

The goal is a relief. City are on our tails in the title race and they're proper Premier League contenders now. They've brought some serious names to the club, like Yaya Touré, David Silva, Edin Dzeko and James Milner. A lot of fans are making out that they're proper title rivals. Scoring a winner as spectacular as that is a real hammer blow to their hopes. From now on, the belief is with us.

*****

PREMIER LEAGUE TABLE, 13 FEBRUARY 2011

	PLAYED	*GD*	*POINTS*
1/ United	26	32	57
2/ Arsenal	26	29	53
3/ City	27	19	49

I'm lucky that my game is based on hard work as well as skill. After a few months back in the first team, the fans can see that I'm giving everything on the football pitch. They know that I'm trying my best. *That I never give up.* Without that attitude, I wouldn't have been able to make it up to the supporters so quickly.

I think that by growing up a passionate football fan myself, I'll always have an appreciation of players that work hard. When I was a kid, if I could see that a footballer like Duncan Ferguson was putting in a shift for Everton, even when the rest of the team wasn't playing great, then I'd always come away thinking, *Well, at least he tried.* I hope the United fans are thinking the same about me.

Look, I admit it, there have been games when we've been losing 3–0 with a minute left on the clock, and I've thought, *Ref, just blow your whistle. Just let us get out of here and get home so we can move on.* But even in those last minutes I never quit, because one goal might come and that could be the difference between winning and losing the Premier League (if it comes down to goal difference). And I couldn't forgive myself if I didn't try my hardest.

*****

Just when I thought I'd worked through the worst of it, I lose my head.

West Ham, Upton Park; 2 April 2011. It's a pressure game, like every match in the Premier League is a pressure game, but we go two goals down – two pens from Mark Noble – and

I feel our strong position at the top of the table slipping away; Arsenal are several points behind us but they have a game in hand. *We cannot lose this game.* Then I score two goals to bring us level; the first a free-kick that curls in from about 25 yards, the second a shot past Rob Green that I set up with a neat touch which takes two defenders out of the game.

Not long afterwards, we win a penalty and I step up to take it. The pressure is unbelievable. It feels like a weight pressing down on me, something heavy sitting on my shoulders, pushing me down into the grass and the mud. My head stays strong.

I will not miss this penalty.

I fire the ball past Green and everything goes blank.

I don't know what's going on.

Suddenly I'm standing by the touchline.

I don't know what's going on.

I can hear the West Ham fans going mental, moaning, yelling.

What's going on?

I start to snap out of it. There are people jumping around me, grabbing me. I can hear a noise. It's me, I'm shouting, screaming. It's as if all the pressure is pouring out. I feel spaced out, lightheaded.

We kill off the game and win 4–2, but as we celebrate in the dressing room, as the goals are being played on a telly in the corner, that's when I see my face for the first time. I'm shouting, screaming and swearing into the cameras.

It's the third goal, those seconds after the penalty. I'm in front of a TV cameraman and shooting my mouth off. It's being beamed into the living rooms of football fans around the country, the world even. My face is all twisted, scowling, angry, wound up. I'm 'effing and blinding.

Oh no.

I sit down at my spot in the dressing room and start to feel sick. I know I've let myself down.

So what do you do now?

Tell them that you didn't know what you were doing?

Yeah right, because that'll sound like a right cop-out when you get asked about it later. But it's the truth, so what else can you say?

Tell them what really happened: that it was such a release to score, that your emotions took over, but you shouldn't have lost it like that.

Hang on, though, it wasn't as if you went looking for the TV cameras so you could gob off. You just got caught up in the moment. Will it be that bad?

I look over at the TV again, watching the action replay, my angry face

Yeah, it'll be bad. Get on with it, Wayne. Apologise.

I collar a club spokesman.

'Look, I need to release a statement,' I say. 'I want to say sorry to anyone who's been offended.'

I put my hands up, but it's not enough. I get banned for two games and everyone's in uproar. The Manager is disappointed, but he knows it was a mistake, that it wasn't intentional. The worst thing is that there are parents on the telly saying I've set a bad example to the kids who were watching.

I think: *As a parent I can understand their opinion, but people do things like that every week playing Sunday League. They get carried away because football is a passionate game. And I've seen parents watching their kids from the touchlines and they're swearing their heads off. It happens all over the country. The difference is of course that they don't have cameras there beaming the pictures into homes all over the world. Another lesson learned.*

I got carried away, made a mistake, and now I regret it and genuinely feel sorry.

I know that if I could turn back the clock, I'd change it, it wouldn't happen. My suspension means that I have to sit out the FA Cup semi-final against City and we lose 1–0. I've made a backwards step.

Convince them to forgive you.

*****

Through all the grief and the negative headlines, I've got to keep calm. United are still in the box seat to win the title and City have fallen away. If we get at least a point against Blackburn in the second to last game of the season, we can wrap up the title.

PREMIER LEAGUE TABLE, 10 MAY 2011

	PLAYED	GD	POINTS
1/ United	36	39	76
2/ Chelsea	36	37	70
3/ Arsenal	36	30	67

But just like the game against West Ham, we make tricky work of it. Our play is nervous, edgy. Blackburn go a goal up after 20 minutes and as the second half slips away, the season looks like going to the final day – a home game against Blackpool, who will probably need to win to have a chance of staying up.

Then with just over a quarter of an hour to go, Javier Hernandez, our Mexican centre-forward, gets upended in the box and all hell breaks loose. Ever since signing for the club in the summer, he's been a livewire. He's always on the move and defenders find it very difficult to track him in the box. This time Blackburn's keeper, Paul Robinson, hauls him down.

The ref blows the whistle, but nobody really knows what's going on, we're not sure if he's given a pen or a goal-kick. Our players are crowding around him; the Blackburn players are crowding around him. They're arguing that the ball had gone out of play before Hernandez was fouled. I don't know what he's going to do but I'm not getting involved.

If he gives it, I don't want to be fired up. I want to be composed, calm. I need to keep my head.

I stand in the penalty area alone and wait for him to decide.

It feels like forever before he makes a call. There's another whistle. The Blackburn players are still arguing, our lot are celebrating. He's pointing to the spot.

Penalty.

You're on.

Ball down.

Now I'm bricking it. There's so much riding on this one kick. It's much worse than the one against West Ham. In fact, I can't remember a time where I've been this nervous on a football pitch before. *If I score, we'll have 17 minutes to see the game out and win the league. Go through your routine, Wayne. The same as always ...*

I look at the ball.

Forget Arsenal.

I look straight at the keeper.

Remember Rangers. Remember West Ham.

I look at the ref.

Once I hear the whistle, I go, head down, and make as sweet a strike as I can.

I keep my nerve and put the ball away. This time, as I celebrate, my mind going blank, I keep my emotions under control. I know we only need a point to win the title. I also know that Blackburn need a point to avoid relegation. With the game tied and everybody happy, nobody's going to do anything silly now. No one's going to push for a winner or take any risks at the back. It's over.

Glory.

When the whistle goes and the players begin to celebrate in the dressing room, one of the coaches shows me some footage on his phone. A fan has posted a video on YouTube. It's a clip of the United supporters in the away end at Blackburn and they're watching as I step up to take the equalising penalty. Except they're not watching; all of them have turned their backs. Some of them are crouching down with their heads in their hands, scared of what might go wrong, like they're watching an entire season flashing before their eyes.

'They look terrified!' someone shouts, looking over my shoulder.

You should have been in my boots, pal.

Then the size of what United have achieved sinks in. *19 league titles.*

That's one more than Liverpool, and as an Evertonian and a United fan it feels mad, satisfying, because it shows what a massive club United are and how much desire we have. It proves how successful The Manager is.

That night, I think about how I want to mark our historic title. I decide on something temporary: I get a pair of scissors and a razor and start shaving into the hair on my chest, shaping it into a reminder for all the United and Liverpool supporters. Then I take a picture of myself and stick it on the social network Twitter. The message is simple:

19

Have that.

*****

CHAMPIONS LEAGUE FINAL, 2011
Manchester United **1** Barcelona **3**
Rooney   Pedro, Messi, Villa

When the Champions League is done and dusted, after we've cruised through the group stages and knocked out Marseille, Chelsea and Schalke; after we've been beaten by one of the greatest club sides of all time in the final at Wembley (the same story as last time: passmovepassmovepassmove), a mate asks me over a game of Xbox one day, 'Would you have won two more Champions Leagues if it wasn't for Barça?'

It's a tough question.

The answer?

'Maybe. But things happen for a reason. They were better than us both times we met them in the final. It just means we have to raise our game against them next time. Watching Messi is mad, though. I see the things he does with a football and I think, *How's he done that?* The tricks he can magic up are incredible.'

Then he asks me how good I think Messi is, you know, compared to the greats like Maradona, Pele, Best ...

'I reckon players get appreciated more when they finish, more than when they're actually playing. But the thing with Messi is that we're watching him now and realising that there's something special happening. Only he can do what he does.'

Doesn't make losing any easier though, does it, Wazza?

'No, I hate losing to them as much as I hate losing to anyone. *Hate it.* The thing is we started off well in the final at Wembley, but then they got a goal. That's when I thought, *Oh, here we go again.* I managed to get an equaliser just before half-time, a cracking strike, but it wasn't enough. In the second half they came out and they were just too good for us. It's tough to take, but they're probably the best club side ever.'

We don't talk about that game again.

The truth is, at the end of the 2010/11 season, despite the Premier League winners' medal and a record 19th league title for my club, there's only one thought going around my head. *I'm so glad it's over.*

CHAPTER

20

FAMILY

Sometimes the biggest changes at a football club can take place in the summer, when there's actually no footy going on. Players come and go; managers come and go. Teams get better (or worse) without anyone kicking a ball about. I can leave Old Trafford for my hols and when I get back everything's changed.

It's never drastic though. Whenever somebody leaves United, the rhythm of football stays the same. The lads just get on with the playing side, The Manager concentrates on picking the team. *It's business as usual.* We're used to squads being chopped about and new faces showing up. I've learned not to be surprised if anyone leaves. Well, anyone apart from The Manager. I can't imagine him being anywhere but United. I was born in 1985 and he took over the dugout a year later. I haven't known Manchester United without him.

Some changes, when they happen, are stranger than others, though. Like Paul Scholes and Gary Nev retiring – Gary in February 2011, Scholesy after the 2010/11 season. Those two have been at the club for as long as I can remember. When I was a kid, I cheered for them both as they turned out for England in the 1998 World Cup and I used to dream of battling against them in an Everton shirt. I can even remember them playing for United against Everton in the 1995 FA Cup final at Wembley.

I knew those two couldn't go on forever, especially Gary. There were games in 2010/11 where he didn't play that well by his high standards. He felt he had a 'mare against West Brom, he didn't play well against Stoke. He made a couple of silly mistakes and I could tell his head was done in by that a bit. Gaz is a proud person, he doesn't want to let himself or United down. After those matches, he must have known the end was coming, that he wasn't good enough for another full season in the first team, so he took the decision out of The Manager's hands and announced his retirement. In a way, he made it easier for the people around him. Typical Gaz, that.

Scholesy's different though, I never saw that one coming at all. He was class on the pitch whenever he played. He calmed the midfield if we were under pressure; there were games where we could have given away silly passes or chucked long balls forward out of panic or desperation. Instead he helped us to retake control in tricky matches. He allowed us to dominate teams and picked out game-changing passes.

I suppose there were a few games when he seemed a little off the pace, but most of the time Scholesy's impact was dead important. We looked a more composed unit with him in the side and I always reckoned he was the complete midfielder – he could pass the ball, shoot, control the tempo of the game; he had the lot. After his announcement The Manager tells the squad that he'll be working as a coach at United, which is a loss for us on the pitch, but I couldn't think of a better person for the younger lads to learn from.

It's funny, I'll probably notice Gary's disappearance from the dressing room much more than Scholesy's, or Edwin van der Sar who's also hung up his boots. Gaz was always a noisy so-and-so in and around the place – having a laugh, making jokes, singing. Paul was the opposite. He was quiet. He just got on with his job. During the week he would come in and train, and as soon as the final whistle had blown in the last practice match, he was in the car and off home. He would have showered and changed before any of us could catch breath.

There's one plus point about Scholesy's retirement, though – it's the fact that I can now breathe a bit easier in training. He was like a terrier in practice games. He would always snap at my ankles whenever I was on the ball, like he did with all the lads; he's always been competitive in the five-a-side games we've had at Carrington and he took that spirit into Premier League matches too, especially when a midfield battle needed winning, or when there was a chance that the other lot might break away and score. He dived into tackles because he was always desperate to win. It was second nature.

I reckon I'm not the only one breathing a sigh of relief as pre-season gets under way though. At the start of our first training session, as the lads get their kit together, I notice that Patrice isn't wearing his shinnies for practice games anymore.

The one player who is still doing it week in, week out, though, is Giggsy. The 2010/11 campaign was a phenomenal season for him, he was top class. He made chances out of nothing, he skinned defenders and worked up and down the flanks like he was a 22-year-old again. In the dressing room, one of the lads tells him he's like Peter Pan because he never seems to get any older. The thing is, he deserves to be playing at the top level at his age because he works really hard to keep fit – he's always pushing himself, stretching, doing yoga to prolong his career. All of us can see Giggsy's desire in training. It's inspirational at times.

Scholes, Gary Nev, Giggsy: I've learned a lot off those three lads during my time here, probably without even knowing it. I've watched some of the things they do in training – their movement, their fitness regimes, the way they prepare themselves; the way they are, their composure in matches – and it's influenced my own game. I've learnt from them in probably the same way that Kai has picked up different mannerisms from me and Coleen whenever we fuss over him, or if we're playing around the house as a family – the faces we pull, the way we laugh. It happens naturally, it's a positive influence. So I can understand why The Manager still wants players like Scholesy around the place. They're important to the group, especially the younger lads – the babies of the club. They're examples of what a player has to do to survive in the modern game.

I suppose a football team is a bit like a family in some ways, too.

*****

There's another change when I get back for pre-season training: I shower, get dressed, and when I look in the mirror, I have a full head of hair for the first time in years. It's a transplant, bits of hair taken from the back of my head and surgically stuck to the front. Despite the comments in a few magazines and the jokes from mates, I think it looks alright.

Some blokes don't mind their hair receding, they're fine with it, but I'll admit that I used to stare at myself in the morning. I used to think, *Bloody hell, you're going bald. You're only a young lad. You don't want to lose all your hair, not in your 20s anyway.*

It never really got me down, but I admit, I found it a bit stressful. Any fella who's lost their hair will know exactly what I mean. It's not fun. I thought about what I was going to do about it. I started looking at myself and thinking, *So why not get a hair transplant?* After a lot of research an appointment was made with the Harley Street Hair Clinic in London.

I'm not soft though. Before the last day of the 2010/11 season, I decide to tell everyone in the dressing room. I know that if I go on holiday with thinning hair and come back looking like Andy Carroll they'll slaughter me over it, especially if it goes wrong, because that's the way footballers are. Nothing's safe at a football club. Everything's a target for a spot of mickey-taking.

New pair of shoes? *Slaughtered.*

Bad picture of you in the paper? *Slaughtered.*

New advert on the telly? *Slaughtered.*

Hair transplant? *Slaughtered.*

When I'm putting my boots away and getting my washbag together after the Blackpool game, I make the announcement.

'Here, I'm going to get a hair transplant done when I go away for the summer ...'

I'm laying down a marker with the lads, like an early tackle on a centre-half. I'm letting them know that I don't care what they think about it, that I'm up for the abuse.

They still slaughter me.

'Oi, Wazza,' someone shouts. 'Are you going to grow a ponytail?'

*****

The 2011/2012 season starts with two batterings. One for us, one for Arsenal. The battering for Arsenal happens first, we spank them 8–2 at home, and it's a game that comes as a massive shock to everyone. To score four past a team as good as Arsenal is some achievement, especially when I think about the success they've had in the past ten, fifteen years. But to score eight? It's unbelievable.

Before the game there's the typical buzz about the place, but nothing unusual is going on. It's not as if The Manager has stumbled across some magic, tactical formula that will help us to tear Arsenal apart. The game basically comes down to form. We've started the season really well, Arsenal have been performing poorly. Our confidence is high and we're playing some great attacking football. Theirs is probably the lowest it's been for years, especially as they've suffered a few injuries in the run-up to the game and one or two of their players have been suspended.

As I sit in the dressing room, I know we're prepared, like we are for any other game, but what happens next is a one-off, a freak game, a match where we look like scoring every time we push into their half.

21 mins: Goal! Danny Welbeck nods the ball in from six yards out.

We're up and running ...

27 mins: Goal! Our new signing Ashley Young fires one into the top right-hand corner from outside the box.

Two now, we just need to keep our heads and put the game out of sight.

40 mins: Goal! I collect the ball on the edge of the area and pass it into the top left-hand corner.

Game over, we'll see the game out in the second half, no probs.

45 mins: they score, Theo Walcott.

OK, no real drama, we're still in control.

63 mins: Goal! I score again, the bottom left-hand side this time, a shot drilled in from the edge of the box.

The away fans have gone quiet, so have the players. Arsenal aren't tackling as hard or working as much as they were in the first 20 minutes …

66 mins: Goal! Nani; I feed him a through ball and he hits it past the keeper from inside their area.

They're all over the place, this lot …

69 mins: Goal! Ji-Sung Park.

Their heads have gone …

73 mins: Arsenal score through Van Persie.

81 mins: Goal! My hat-trick, a pen.

They've given up. They don't have the fight …

90 mins: Goal! Ashley Young curls one into the top right-hand corner from the edge of the box.

The final whistle goes. The Arsenal lot look relieved, pleased that it's over …

It's a mad score, and one that doesn't happen that often in the Premier League. It's so unexpected that I even feel sorry for them (a bit), because being on the end of a result like that is horrible, sick, embarrassing. Like when we were spanked 4–1 by Middlesbrough in 2005. I couldn't wait for the final whistle to blow. I wanted to get out of there as quickly as I could. *I never want to go through that again.*

But then it happens to us; it's our turn to get hammered. *City.*

They batter us 6–1, but it's even worse than the Boro' result because it happens at Old Trafford, in front of our own fans. It's also a massacre that could so easily have been avoided.

We start off alright, but City score in the first half through Mario Balotelli. Then Jonny Evans gets sent off just after half-time and that's when it all goes wrong. I know we're in trouble because getting the ball off City's players is hard enough with 11 men, they keep it so well.

It's going to be a right mission now.

It's no surprise to anyone when they score two more, but when we pull a goal back with 10 minutes to go through Fletch, I still have the belief that we might get back into the game. *If we can hang on here, you never know. A second might put the wind up them and put a bit of pressure on …*

They bang in three at the death.

Gutted.

We always knew that City would be serious title rivals this season. They've fallen away in campaigns over the past couple of years, but I can tell they've got some proper quality in the side now – their new signing, Argentinian striker Sergio Aguero's different class up front; Yaya Touré is a monster in the middle of the park. And in Joe Hart they probably have one of the best goalkeepers in the world. They look stronger than ever before.

It's hard to take. We sit in the dressing room afterwards staring at our feet. No one wants to shower. There's silence, awkward coughing. Somebody kicks a water bottle across the room. The younger lads in the squad, like Danny Welbeck, Phil Jones – who we signed from Blackburn in the summer, a strong player – and Chris Smalling, look shell-shocked. But so do the older heads. I know a game like this can be damaging to a young player's confidence, especially if they haven't experienced it before; the more senior lads can't let the rot set in.

We have to get over it.

'Listen, it's happened,' I say, to no one and everyone. 'We have to move on. It's only three points, let's pick ourselves up and win the next few games. This 6–1 thrashing is a freak, like the Arsenal game. A one-off.'

I know it's not much, but it's better than saying nothing.

*****

When I leave Old Trafford after the game against Arsenal, I hear The Manager giving an interview to someone from one of the TV stations. He's telling him that he wanted the scoring to stop during the 8–2 win over Arsenal. Apparently, he didn't want to humiliate Arsene Wenger's side any more.

I have a laugh to myself as I walk to the coach. All we hear in training, in pre-match meetings, before the kick-off, at half-time and even at full-time, is: 'Score as many as you can, lads. Keep going, try to finish teams off and get more goals.'

I know what The Manager means, but our job as players is to score goals and win games. After all, you never know, the title could come down to goal difference one year.

*****

I can't wait to play City again.

I want to beat them so badly.

I want to prove that the result at Old Trafford isn't the first sign of a changing balance of power.

It's December when I get the news that we're playing them in the FA Cup Third Round at their place.

Looking forward to it already.

*****

In the league, we get back on track.

Everton 0	Manchester United 1
Manchester United 1	Sunderland 0
Swansea 0	Manchester United 1
Manchester United 1	Newcastle 1
Villa 0	Manchester United 1
Manchester United 4	Wolves 1
QPR 0	Manchester United 2
Fulham 0	Manchester United 5
Manchester United 5	Wigan 0

The squad's pulling together; we're sitting in second place behind City in the table and everyone at the club is getting behind the first team. Even Paul Scholes is doing full training sessions with the reserves rather than coaching them from the sidelines. *What's he doing that for? Doesn't look like much of a retirement from playing to me. Not if you're going to be working as hard as the rest of us.*

I do my bit by dropping into a central midfield role when the team gets hit by injuries. The Manager thinks I can do a job there and with the likes of Tom Cleverley, Anderson, Michael Carrick and Fletch all missing games, he asks me to help out. When I get stuck into the action as a central play-maker, I love it. I get more of the ball, I'm involved loads and after one game I even think about playing there permanently (but only later on in my career).

Why? Well, in midfield I don't have to be as sharp as a forward. I have to focus my energy on moving from box to box instead. But as a striker I'm always making quick runs, I use short bursts of pace. Once I feel that I haven't got the sharpness needed to get away from defenders, I'll probably drop back into midfield for a couple of seasons so I can still influence the game.

In my heart I know I'd prefer it if I was playing upfront because I can still do a lot of damage in the box, but the sacrifices don't bother me. I'm happy at United, despite the downs that sometimes take place at a football club. Like when we stuff Wigan 5–0 on Boxing Day. I go out for dinner with a few of the lads and our other halves to a hotel. The next day The Manager pulls me up and tells me he's not happy and doesn't feel I've trained properly. He fines me, but there's worse to come. I'm dropped for the next game against Blackburn. At a lot of clubs, people wouldn't bat an eyelid at players having a night out six days before a game; but that's the difference at United and a mark of the high standards The Manager demands. It's a big deal; another lesson learned. The following week, I sit in the stands and watch us lose 3–2 to Blackburn. It's the worst feeling. They're terrible, they look certs for relegation; we're more terrible than them. As I follow the match, I feel desperate, helpless like the other fans watching the defeat unfold in front of us.

It's no fun being a supporter sometimes …

✳✳✳✳✳

City, the FA Cup Third Round.

It's the morning of the game and in the team hotel, United coach Paul Scholes is standing in his United suit, tie, smart shirt and polished shoes. It's funny to see him as a coach and not a player these days, but it's also nice of him to show up so he can give the lads a bit of support. As a footballer, it sometimes helps to have a calm head on the bus for an away game, especially a match as big as this one.

An hour later, as we sit in the away team dressing room, I notice Scholesy stripping out of his fancy clobber. He's putting on a warm-up top, the one that's been hanging up alongside the other kits for the first team. That's when I see the shirt for the first time:

Scholes
22

I start looking around at everyone else, to make sure I'm not the only one who's noticed what's going on. The lads are staring at him, jaws on the deck. Scholesy doesn't say a word to anyone, as usual. He's pulling on his shorts, ignoring the fuss around him. There's shouting, cheering. The squad's buzzing. The younger lads like Chris Smalling can't believe they're going to be playing with one of the best midfielders United has ever known.

'Eh? When did this happen?'

'The Manager's kept that one quiet!'

I can't get my head around it.

One of United's best midfielders for years is back to play against City in the FA Cup and none of us have been told? You couldn't make this up …

We beat City 3–2; I score a couple. It goes some way to paying them back for the hammering they gave us at the start of the season; Scholesy comes on in the second half to a massive cheer, but he makes a mistake that gives City a goal.

It's no big drama in the end though. The game is ours and I know his match legs will come back. His return can only be a good thing, and it feels like a new signing for us, like a family reunion.

*****

Not for everyone.

Tuesday morning is the first day of training after our win against City. When I look down at Patrice's legs as he walks out for training, I notice a pair of shinnies have been stuffed back into his socks. *So we're not all chuffed that Scholesy's back, then.*

CHAPTER

21

OFFICE

An hour before the league game against Liverpool, February 2012. I wait in my office. Well, it's not an office really, but it's the closest thing I have to one: the dressing room underneath the South Stand at Old Trafford, a room tucked away in the far corner of the ground.

In a way, it's a bit like most offices. Meetings take place here and decisions get sorted. There's gossip, banter and a few unwritten rules: like never, ever speak when The Manager's angry. My workplace is somewhere along the back wall where a Manchester United shirt hangs from a peg with the number 10 and 'Rooney' printed on the back. Underneath it are my shorts, socks, shinnies and footy boots, all laid out in a pile.

I'm not the only one here. Seventeen other people – Giggsy, Rio, Antonio Valencia, Michael Carrick, Jonny Evans and the rest – are doing the same thing as me. They hang around their spots, mess about in their lockers and go through their usual routines, superstitions, habits, like it's just another day at work.

At first it's quiet, but it doesn't take long for things to liven up a bit. Patrice Evra plugs his iPod into a dock; R&B bangs out from the speakers. The jokes start flying around, some of the lads are having a crack. Michael Carrick and Scholesy play two touch with a ball, kicking it backwards and forwards across the floor. Rio's taking the mickey out of Patrice's clothes, hanging them up for everyone to laugh at. In a room next door, Valencia gets on one of six exercise bikes and starts his warm-up.

I sit down and begin to focus. There's 58 minutes to wait until kick-off.

Too much time.

I undress and pull on my shorts.

I feel good; not nervous, just ready. Moments earlier I was buzzing around the players' lounge, trying to relax. I felt edgy then, but now the game's so close, I go quiet. It's a weird habit I've had since I started playing as a kid. I've always gone into my shell as a kick-off gets closer, I don't want to talk to anyone, I don't get involved in the messing around. I'd much rather keep myself to myself.

Get your head straight for the match instead.

I change into my socks, training top and boots.

I hop on the massage table before Michael Carrick can get there and the club masseur, Rod 'The Rub' goes to work on my thighs. I groan as he grips and pulls at my legs but I can feel the blood flow increasing and the muscles getting warmer. *Pain turning into heat turning into strength.*

I start to picture the next 90 minutes and how they might go for me. Like the pre-match visualisation I always go through in a hotel room the night before a game, I imagine goals and positive passes; great tackles; flashes of skill turning defenders inside out.

I get on the bike and pedal, feeling the muscles in my calves starting to loosen, my heart rate getting faster. I'm seeing goals in my head, 20 yarders flying past Liverpool goalkeeper Pepe Reina. I imagine popping the ball through defender Daniel Agger's legs, rounding him and dinking the ball over the advancing keeper.

I look up at the telly in the office. *Sky Sports News* is on, they're going through the usual build-up to today's game. My eyes drift over to the clock alongside it. There's ages to go, 52 minutes.

Too much time.

The second hand's moving so slowly, like someone's messed about with it.

I get off the bike, wishing the seconds away. I can hear a weird muffled hum. It's the buzz of the fans outside in the ground. There's the occasional shout of 'United!', laughter, whistles.

I want the match to start.

I pull on my training top and boots. I grab a ball and head out for the warm-up, through the long and dark tunnel; narrow, cramped, going on for miles and miles. Past the ball boys and the police and the coaches; under the red canopy that stretches onto the grass, into the bright green blur of the pitch, the sun; the noise and the hum and the buzz getting louder, sharper. There's a cheer, applause as we jog onto the park. Then the ground starts singing.

'United! United!'

Because Liverpool are here, there's a real atmosphere about Old Trafford today. The crowd are up for it. So am I. A lot of people have been banging on about the fact that I've not scored as many goals against this lot as I should have done. Maybe that's because I've always 'disliked' them (The Manager's word, not mine) as an Everton fan and I always want to beat them so badly. I never scored against them in the Merseyside derby. My mates reckon I try too hard.

We stretch and pass, jog and stretch and shoot and stretch. I see more goals in my head. I imagine the youth club pitch back in Croxteth, The Goals, Gems, the torn netting, the floodlights.

I wonder what it looks like now?

Then I get the feeling – the same one I experience before every game of football.

Today I'm going to score.

*****

There's a back story to this game.

When we played Liverpool at their place earlier on in the season it all kicked off: Patrice and Liverpool's Uruguayan striker, Luis Suarez, got involved in a row. I was nowhere near the incident when it happened, but apparently there were words as the pair of them went in for a corner. From where I was standing, I could see they were rucking over something, but I didn't have a clue what.

When we got into the dressing room at full-time, Patrice went mad.

'He racially abused me!' he shouted. He was furious, wound up.

After the game there were allegations; people were saying this, that and the other about the incident, and everyone was up in arms about it. The matter was referred to the FA and a hearing was held in December. The FA decided that Suarez was guilty and in a statement they said that his actions had 'damaged the image of English football around the world'.

When I heard the result of the hearing I felt relief for Patrice as it vindicated him, but I was also sure of something else.

It's going to be a needle game the next time we play Liverpool …

*****

By the time the game comes around, everyone's asking one thing: will Patrice shake Luis Suarez's hand in the line-up before kick-off? As I warm up with short sharp sprints, then some shooting practice, I can feel an edginess building in the ground.

I haven't got a clue what's going to happen here today.

*****

We're called back to the dressing room.

It's nearly time.

The Manager comes in to give his team talk. Because Liverpool are such a big deal at any stage of the season, this is the second time he's delivered a briefing on their lot in 24 hours. He reminds us of how important the match is. He shows us again where we should be for free-kicks. He tells us who to mark on corners. He tells us how he wants us to play.

'Squeeze them,' he says. 'If we can defend high up the pitch and play in their half, then we can get them on the back foot.'

'One more thing lads ... keep your heads out there today. Forget what happened last time, just deal with the game in front of you. If you stay focused you'll get all three points.'

He leaves the room without saying anything else. I think of my instructions on corners: stick on Reina in goal, don't let him get to those crosses.

I put my shinnies on.

I put my match shirt on.

I go to the toilet and pee.

I go to the physio's room alone, sit on the bed and pray.

Let me get through the 90 minutes safely; let me have an injury-free game.

I'm not sure if anyone else prays before games. I suppose we have a lot of different nationalities and cultures at United, so some of the lads might be doing it now, too. But if anyone else is praying, then they're doing it in their own way. All I know is that praying helps me to focus, to keep calm.

I get back to my seat. Patrice is talking to everyone. He says, 'I'm going to shake his hand. It's the sporting thing to do.'

Everyone agrees.

Fair play mate – that's being the bigger man.

I take a look at how he is, his confidence. The Manager has named him as skipper today. He's a good leader, Patrice.

He's relaxed, given what's happened. He's a bit quieter than usual, but he's focused. Well, how would you be? You've been in games where you've played against someone you've had run-ins with before …

I tighten the laces on my boots one last time.

… The same probably. Though it's easy for you to say, 'Come on, Patrice, just get on with the game today. Put it behind you, lad.'

I snap back.

Focus, Wayne.

My concentration is only broken when the buzzer goes, an alarm that tells the players it's time to line up in the tunnel.

I'm ready now.

Today we're going to win and I'm going to score.

*****

Suarez won't play ball.

In the team line-up before the game, the Liverpool lot walk alongside the United players to shake hands. Patrice is at the front. He's doing the captain's bit.

Here comes Suarez …

This is the moment people have been talking about all week …

Patrice sticks out his hand to greet him, to put things behind them, but Suarez isn't interested. Instead he reaches for the bloke next to him, our goalie David de Gea.

He hasn't taken it!

He's ignored him. Patrice looks dead moody about it, too.

He comes to me, I shake his hand instinctively, a bit confused by it all.

That won't look so good for Suarez. He'll probably regret that later down the line. Why couldn't he just shake his hand so we can get on with the football?

The players run into their halves for a final stretch, a last-minute touch of the ball. There are boos, whistling, everyone in the crowd is going mad.

Forget it, Wayne. Today we're going to win and you're going to score.

*****

Half-time, 0–0. It's anyone's game.

I walk back to the tunnel, trying to take in what's happened in those 45 minutes; the chances, the tackles, trying to second guess what The Manager's going to say.

When I get to the corridor that leads to the dressing rooms, I can't get through. The police have blocked it off. I can see there's a bit of pushing and shoving in the distance, but I can't make out between who. There are coaches dragging players into the dressing rooms, calming everything down. Me and Stevie Gerrard are standing behind a gang of police waiting, like a right pair of soft lads.

When I get back in the office, The Manager has calmed everyone; he's telling us to keep the tempo high. I look around trying to work out what's happened but everyone's focused on The Manager. I haven't got a clue what's happened in the tunnel.

'We're in the match,' he's saying. 'Keep going at them, push them back. Keep the pace of the game high and we'll get a goal, maybe two.'

Our half-time team talks are always different – I never know what to expect. I've gone in when we've been winning three-nil, but The Manager has gone crazy. Sometimes I dread half-time if we're hammering a team because I know he doesn't want complacency, so we're going to get rollicked.

If we're playing badly but winning 1–0 at the break, he'll get angry with us. He doesn't want the opposition to come back at us in the second half and nick a point. Other times, when we've been losing by a goal, he'll just tell us to carry on the way we are. He knows an equaliser is coming. His experience tells him that sometimes United won't play well, but we can still win.

The scariest times are when we're losing and not playing well. I have to stay quiet as much as I can during those meetings. If I open my mouth at the wrong time and upset The Manager, I'll be in big trouble. Answering back is intimidating and scary. A bad move. Afterwards it's always forgotten though, and after a telling off, he won't even speak about it the next day, like it didn't even happen. I guess he's too busy thinking about how we're going to win the next game.

There's no shouting today. After our team talk, the backroom staff go to work. The fitness coaches give out energy bars, gels and drinks. We have Coco Pops bars and Jaffa Cakes for anyone feeling tired. I need a sugar hit. Mick Phelan and René Meulensteen, our coaches, talk to the players one-on-one. They tell us the things they've noticed about the game and how Liverpool are shaping up. Mick sits down next to me. He reckons I could work their back four harder.

'Don't just stand up behind the defenders,' he says. 'Try to pin Skrtel and Agger back and create space for our midfielders.'

I nod.

I gulp down my energy drink, eat my Jaffa Cake, and think about scoring. Scoring and winning.

*****

I score; second half, 46th minute.

A cracking volley straight past Reina.

A few minutes later I score again.

Not many things feels better than scoring against Liverpool.

We win, 2–1.

Suarez gets theirs, but it's not enough to dampen the mood as the team buzzes around the office afterwards. There's a queue for the food, which is a good sign. When United have won, everyone heads straight for the table loaded up with pizzas, fajita wraps and potato wedges, pushing, shoving, laughing, like they do today. We all get stuck in. It's noisy, everyone's dead chuffed.

Then Patrice puts the iPod back on – he's buzzing, the fuss over the handshake already forgotten. This time it's Brazilian party music, Samba stuff. It's great in here after a win.

If we lose, it's totally different. Following a defeat – like the 6–1 against City – no one touches the food. There's a deathly silence. It's like being in church. Defeat is the worst.

If I know we haven't played well and we've deserved to lose, I always have a weird sinking feeling inside. I feel sorry for myself, I feel like we've let everyone down. I feel embarrassed.

Even if I've played well personally but we've lost, it's no consolation. I might have scored two goals in a game, but if we've been beaten 3–2, I feel bad afterwards. It's not bitter-sweet, it's horrible.

Not today though. Today we've won and I've scored a couple of goals. More importantly, we've beaten Liverpool and we're still in the hunt for the title. Somebody takes the mickey out of a chance I scuffed late in the game. Scholesy cheekily stepped over the ball. It was a neat dummy that gave me a great chance to get my hat-trick. Instead I fired the ball wide.

I make out that I meant it.

'I was trying to play a one-two with the post, but I missed,' I shout back.

I feel good. I get stuck into my potato wedges. I listen to Patrice's Samba music on the stereo. I wonder how City will get on tomorrow against Villa. I think about our next game against Norwich. And the game after that against Spurs.

Then I think about scoring more goals, winning more games.

CHAPTER

22

MARGINS

Talk about ups and downs.

In the 2011/12 season, I make my 500th senior appearance, but then I'm making all sorts of records and personal achievements. Like on 10 September 2011, when I get three goals in a 5–0 win over Bolton and become only the fourth player in Premier League history to score back-to-back hat-tricks (it follows those three goals in the 8–2 thrashing of Arsenal). Or on 18 October 2011, when I score two goals against Otelul Galati in the Champions League group stages and it takes me past Scholesy as the highest-scoring Englishman in the history of the Champions League.

I even have my best season for yellow cards. I only get one all campaign because I work hard on the silly bookings I usually pick up every year. I keep my mouth shut when refs give decisions against us. I don't react to players when they try to wind me up.

I can feel my temperament changing. Some people might think it's down to the incident at West Ham or my terrible year in 2010/11, but really it's more likely to be a result of my age. I've grown up loads recently and as I've got older, I've become calmer. People forget that I've been in the limelight since I was 16. Back then my emotions were all over the place, like they would be for any teenager. Even four or five years ago, when I was in my early 20s, my enthusiasm and short fuse was probably down to immaturity. I was reckless on the pitch, desperate to make every tackle, every pass, because I was so mad on winning. If ever someone said anything to me or my teammates in the heat of a game, I'd usually react badly in one way or another. I'd give it back or jump into the next tackle too quickly. I was like a firework waiting to go off.

I guess it's normal to be wound up at that age. People have so much energy, too much sometimes. Add that to a lack of maturity and it becomes a dangerous mix. I know because I've gone through that stage. I'd like to think that it's over and done with for me now.

Well, nearly over and done with. The thing is, I know I'm still prone to the odd rush of blood to the head. My red card in October 2011, when England play Montenegro in a European Championship qualifier, is an example of that. During the game, my head goes. I lash out at a player with my boot after I lose control of the ball and I get sent off. It means I have to miss the first two games of the finals in Poland and Ukraine.

So, there's still a bit of work to do then.

The most important thing is that by calming my emotions down, my game is actually benefiting. I'm not chasing the ball all over the pitch, I'm saving my energy for the opponent's half instead. I'm focusing on working in and around the box; I'm being more selfish, especially when it comes to taking my chances in front of goal. Don't get me wrong, if someone's in a better position than me, I'll always pass the ball to them. But if the keeper's beat and the ball's coming back across goal, then I'll always try to be the first one in – before Berba, Hernandez, or Danny Welbeck can get there. It's a striker's mindset. *I love scoring goals.*

I get loads of them in the second half of the 2011/12 season and every one of them is a buzz at the time, but by the end of the campaign they mean nothing. The personal records mean nothing. The improved temperament means nothing. And you want to know why?

Because we get knocked out of the League Cup quarter-final by Crystal Palace.

We get knocked out of the FA Cup Fourth Round by Liverpool.

We don't even make it through the group stage of the Champions League. And then we get knocked out of the Europa League by Atletico Bilbao.

Who cares how many personal accolades a player picks up in a season if they've not got a trophy to show for it at the end?

I don't.

*****

There's still the Premier League.

In April, we build an eight-point gap between us and City with six games to go. We're in the driving seat and everyone's thinking the same thing, including me.

This is United, we know what we're doing. We'll see this out.
But we don't.

We face Wigan away. They're playing some good football despite being stuck in the bottom three for large chunks of the season. From the kick-off, the momentum seems to be with them and everything goes against us. They score from a corner, though it should have been a goal-kick; the ref turns down a penalty appeal by us. We can't seem to get behind their defence and make chances.

Games like this do my head in, matches when I can't work out what's going wrong, why we're not clicking.

We could be playing for five hours straight here and still not score. As it's happening, I can see that the whole team is locked into the same mad mindset, but there's nothing we can do to snap out of it.

The fans can sense it in these games too. They can tell we're not going to put one away. Frustration starts to creep in as the game goes on, and the players try that much harder. That increased pressure leads to more mistakes and Wigan take control of the game. The only answer is to keep going, to push the opposition back.

Maybe a lucky pen or a deflected goal will change the mood.

It doesn't happen for us. Wigan win 1–0. We deserve it. They play well, we play poorly. Our eight-point lead becomes five.

We play Everton at home and go 4–2 up; I score a couple – my goals take me past George Best and Dennis Viollet on United's list of all-time scorers (I go fourth). Nani and Danny Welbeck get goals as well and I can feel I've really built up a good understanding with Danny. He's quick, he's great when he's running in behind defences and he's good with his feet. I love it when he comes short, pulling the defence with him because he can link the play up with me and the midfield. It allows me to get behind the back four.

But just when everything's going well against Everton, something unexpected happens. We relax. We act like the game's won. We give their wide men, like winger Steven Pienaar, too much time on the ball and they punish us. They hit crosses into the box towards their two target men, Marouane Fellaini and Nikica Jelavic. Everton get two late goals from Jelavic and Pienaar and snatch a 4–4 draw.

Disaster. Five points becomes three.

Then it's crunch time: City at their place and it feels like a cup final. Everything seems to rest on this game. I know that if we beat them we'll go into the last two games of the season with a six-point cushion, which should give us the title, psychologically at least. They know that if they beat us, they'll draw level, but it will edge them ahead on goal difference.

It's a big ask to win this game. City are strong, solid, especially at home, and in the 45th minute their captain, Vincent Kompany, scores a header from a corner. After that we can't break them down. They keep the ball away from us and dominate possession. We can't even pop a shot off at goal. I don't think Joe Hart has a save to make for the rest of the game.

We lose, 1–0.

PREMIER LEAGUE TABLE, 30 APRIL 2012

	PLAYED	GD	POINTS
1/ City	36	61	83
2/ United	36	53	83
3/ Arsenal	36	24	66

Eight points to nothing in the blink of an eye.

*****

I keep asking the same question over and over. *Second on goal difference? How has this happened?*

The experts start having a pop at us, they're saying we've blown it. People are going on about how good City are, how they play great football, how they're the strongest team in the league. They're also saying that we're a below-average United team and we're not as good as some of The Manager's sides of the past. *Well, if that's the case, how come we're only behind City on goal difference?*

It couldn't be any closer.

Everyone's on edge.

If there's one person who knows how we feel, then it's Gary Nev. He's on the TV quite a lot and he's saying the same thing over and over again: 'If United lose this title on goal difference, The Manager will hate it more than anything, because it's a nightmare to have the same points as the champions and not to have your hands on the trophy. There's nothing worse in the game.'

He's spot on there.

I try to think of why we've gone wrong, how we've given away so many silly goals in games we ordinarily would have won. I think we've been naive sometimes. Normally we'd close games out. The draw with Everton was a match that we never would have chucked away before, but instead of killing the game off, we pushed forward and looked to attack; we left ourselves exposed. We forgot about the importance of winning games by the odd goal, and when we went ahead at 2–1, then 3–1, then 4–2 (they scored first), we tried to grab more goals rather than shutting up shop as The Manager would have liked.

It was the same in the Champions League. We dropped points in matches we should have sewn up. We showed a lack of experience against Basle and Benfica at home in the group – tough games, but games we should have taken all three points from. On those nights we forgot to defend all over the pitch. We just wanted to attack the other lot.

I know I've been guilty of that myself in the past, so I can see it when other players forget about defending. When I was in my teens and my early 20s, all I thought about was scoring goals. I wanted to score all the time. I wanted to push forward and attack whenever I got the opportunity. Now I've realised I can't do that in the Champions League or the Premier League. A good team will always punish us if ever we get carried away. And we've done it too many times this season, in both the league and Europe.

Now it's cost us, big time.

*****

The Manager can see it, too. Following our defeat to Wigan, we beat Villa 4–0. I score two goals, one of them a pen, but again the team doesn't play that well, despite the scoreline. The Manager has a pop at me after the game. He says to the media afterwards: 'Wayne has to play on the edge of a game, when it's really close and competitive. When the game gets to that casual bit, he's worse than the rest of them. He gets really casual about it. It's better when he's on the edge. Then he's a marvellous player.'

I don't complain. I think he's trying to keep us all on our toes as the season gets to the business end. He has to. There's no room for error.

*****

After the defeat at the Etihad Stadium we beat Swansea 2–0 at home; City beat Newcastle 2–0 at St James' Park. It's all coming down to the last game of the season.

PREMIER LEAGUE TABLE, 6 MAY 2012

	PLAYED	GD	POINTS
1/ City	37	63	86
2/ United	37	55	86
3/ Arsenal	37	24	67

We train well all week. The Manager gets us focused on the match ahead. He tells us the Premier League is City's to lose rather than ours to win; they have QPR at home, we have Sunderland away. Everyone expects City to pick up a comfortable three points. He says that all we can do is to win our match and pray that QPR can upset the odds and pull off a shock result.

The good thing is, Rangers will be up for this game. They're two points ahead of Bolton in the relegation zone and need a result to ensure their safety 100%; if Bolton lose or draw their match at Stoke, QPR will be fine regardless. *This is the closest end to a season I've ever known.*

Then The Manager tells us to expect the unexpected.

'If it happens, if City blow it, it won't be the first time things haven't gone the way we thought, lads,' he says one lunchtime as everyone sits down to eat in the club canteen. 'In 1995, we played West Ham away and Blackburn were playing Liverpool. Blackburn had to win to guarantee them the title; if they drew and we won, we'd win the league. Nobody expected Liverpool to do United a favour by beating Blackburn, but they did. The only problem was that we drew with West Ham in the end, so Blackburn finished at the top of the Premier League.

'I don't want that to happen again. So do your job and beat Sunderland. Let the rest take care of itself.'

I try to shut everything out. I make out to myself that it's a normal week because I know that over-thinking, focusing on what could go wrong, is bad news for a sportsman. Like if a golfer stands at the tee box and visualises the massive bunker in the middle of the fairway rather than the acres of green grass in front of him. Chances are, he's finding the sand. I know that if I go into the Sunderland game worrying about the outcome, or thinking about not playing well, then it's going to mess with my head.

Stay upbeat. Think about scoring goals, playing well.

Do your job.

*****

When it comes to the game, we start well. We do our job.

I score first to put us in top spot. Then City go ahead at the Etihad – their defender, Pablo Zabaleta, gets one just before half-time. It's mad, when City score and the news flies around the ground, our fans fall silent, like we've conceded the goal ourselves.

For a while there, we were top of the table.

But it's not over yet. After 47 minutes QPR do the unthinkable and equalise. The United end at The Stadium of Light goes mental. Twenty minutes later, Rangers do the impossible for a second time and go 2–1 up. Our fans are losing it, the players can sense the league is coming back to Old Trafford. I can't make out what's going on, nobody can. *Is it over? Have City really blown it?*

When the final whistle goes there's complete confusion. I'm looking to the bench, trying to work out whether we're champions. Everyone's staring at one another, shrugging their shoulders. Phil Jones looks completely stunned, lost. Then the Sunderland fans start cheering. They're turning their backs to the ground and bouncing up and down.

That's 'The Poznan' – the celebration that City do whenever they score; the celebration they copied off that Polish team, Lech Poznań. Oh god, City are champions …

The Manager is walking towards us. He's telling us to thank the fans. My heart sinks. I can see it's done, finished. Someone shouts, 'City scored two in injury time' and I feel sick. I jog to our end of the ground, the fans applauding us as we go over to see them. They look heartbroken. *We know how you feel.* Then I look towards the Sunderland supporters and they're made up, laughing. *What, because we've lost out on the title at the last minute? Why are they so bothered about us?*

I think about playing Sunderland next season, beating them, because focusing on anything other than City, however small, goes some way to making me feel better. But only for a split second.

*****

That night, I live through the pain again.

Match of the Day on the telly.

Some players can't watch themselves playing on the box when they've lost, but I can. I have to watch. I have to see what I've done wrong. Tonight is weird though, because we've won, I've scored, but I'm still a loser. I've come second.

I settle down in front of the telly and take in the madness. Coleen leaves me to it. She knows I'll be grumpy for a while, and as I stare at the box, as the cameras move from the Etihad to The Stadium of Light, I can't believe how the day has unfolded.

At City, QPR's captain Joey Barton gets sent off.

Great. That's them with an advantage.

I watch as QPR go 2–1 up.

How did they manage that?

Then I see us winning at Sunderland.

Well, we did our job.

As things stand, we're champions, but only on the telly, and that means nothing because there's no pause button for the Premier League – I can't freeze the table with us still in first place.

The cameras show the confusion at Sunderland, The Manager looking around, and now everything's about to change for the worst because City have their five minutes of injury time to play. Five minutes that will change the shape of the league, and even though I know what's coming, I can't look away. I'm like a driver staring at a car crash on the motorway.

I can see City's fans. A load of them are crying as their game goes on. They think their team are throwing it away, it's that close to the end for them. The clock says 91 minutes, and that's when City score; Edin Dzeko, 2–2.

And here it comes, the killer blow …

On 93 minutes, Aguero scores again, City get their winner. We lose out; City get their title.

I turn the TV off.

Silence.

Gary Neville was right. There's nothing worse than having the same points as the champions but being second best.

Coleen's in bed. There's not a sound in the house. I want to go up too, to sleep, to shut it all out. But I know it's the worst thing for me because my mind is going in circles. Round and round, over and over; action replays, Manchester United games in slow motion. I'm re-living missed chances, disallowed penalties, opportunities that were called offside. *How can I sleep tonight when all I can think about are the goals we could have scored?*

*****

When the dust settles, it's the same old story. It happens every year.

United are finished. They won't win the league for a while now.

According to some fans, we haven't got a hope of taking the title in the coming season or two. It can't be done because apparently City are the best team around. Chelsea too. They win the Champions League on penalties against Bayern

Munich. By all accounts they're ahead of us in the pecking order as well now.

Fair enough, but people have short memories. They were writing us off before my first season at the club in 2004, and they've said it every season since. In that time, I've won four titles. Not bad for a no-hope team with no chance.

Maybe it's wishful thinking on the part of other people. Maybe fans of other clubs love to write us off because they're sick of United winning all the time. I don't know. I don't care. I learnt one thing when I first turned up at this place: *Never count us out.*

EPILOGUE

90 MINUTES (PLUS FERGIE TIME)

Training, Carrington, any given day; the usual routine. The Manager's Audi in the car park; a walk through the club reception with its fancy model of Old Trafford in the foyer. Down a brightly lit corridor, past the photos on the wall of the famous Busby Babes, Giggsy and Ronaldo; The Manager looking scary in a smart suit. Through more doors, into the mess and banter of the dressing room.

Every day, I see the same thing as I walk in: a massive framed picture of the Champions League-winning team of 2008. It's hanging from a wall that overlooks the treatment table and it's a reminder of a brilliant moment in my life. Everyone's on the pitch in Moscow, spraying champagne about, laughing, smiling, *buzzing*. Carlos Tevez has a grin the size of a Cheshire Cat. Ronaldo's hair looks immaculate, even though it's tipping it down with rain and there's confetti everywhere.

I love that photo. Every time I see it, usually as I'm getting ready to stretch, sprint, work, I always think the same thing.

That's the excitement of football right there. I think I love it so much because I understand that it's an experience most footballers won't get at the highest level. It makes me feel lucky. Blessed.

But how many more of those moments have I got to come?

A decade is a long time for most people, but in footy it feels like a heartbeat because everything flies by so quickly – every game, every goal, every tackle. There's no rewind or pause button for a footballer, not when the focus is always on the next game, the next three points, *the future.* Because of that I've always looked ahead, I've never been in the moment, and everything's whizzed by. In a flash, I'm nearer to 30 than 20; I'm talked about as a senior player at United. I've learned hard lessons. *I've got experience.*

It's dead mad. Inside I'm still the same kid with a bowl haircut and bandy legs who was turning out for the school team at 14 years of age, all enthusiasm and energy. The excitement and the adrenaline I now feel as I walk onto the pitch at Old Trafford is the same as when I was a kid playing for the school team. The buzz is there, only the size of the games have changed. Instead of leading out Copplehouse Boys' Club, I'm lining up for the biggest team in the world and there's nothing better. Playing in the Premier League, scoring goals and winning trophies for the fans? It's what drives me on every single day.

There's one difference, though. At that time, in the beginning, I couldn't imagine *not* playing football. I couldn't see the end in sight. I never pictured a time when I wouldn't be getting my head straight before a match, psyching myself up, lacing my footy boots.

It's different now. I'm about to hit my peak in the game and I feel strong. I'm improving and learning every single day, but I know the end may be nearer than the start. A football life is a dead short one, so I'm trying to enjoy every pass, every goal, every tackle now, because it won't last forever. *From now on, I need to live in the moment, just a little bit.*

The Manager probably feels the same way. I reckon it's why he's stayed on at the club for so long – he's been here for over 25 years. If he can manage United at the top level and win, feel the buzz, then why would he want to retire? There's a rush every time we land trophies together at United; a shot of excitement so mad that it takes a while to calm down. I feel it every time. But the second that sensation begins to disappear – about two or three weeks afterwards – I need to chase the next hit. I want to be battling for success again and again and again. The craving is strong because winning is such a great feeling. *He must get that too.*

There have been loads of highs, loads of top moments during my decade in the Premier League. The title in 2006/07 will always feel like the best one because it was the first. I admit it, having gone two seasons at United without it – and having watched a strong Chelsea team do so well in the league – I thought we might not win the Premier League, not for a while anyway. It was frustrating, especially as it was the reason I'd left Everton. *To be a title winner.* Once I got the first, I knew I'd get loads more.

The Champions League win was incredible as well; Moscow will live with me forever – the penalty shootout, the drama, the tension. Then there's the goals over the years – that overhead kick against City, my goal for Everton against Arsenal, the penalty against Blackburn that won United the league in 2011. Those split seconds are stuck in my head for good.

I'd be lying if I made out that there weren't lows to match the highs. Red cards and bookings. Injuries. FA Cup final defeats, losing out to Barça in the Champions League final twice, losing the Premier League to City on goal difference in 2012. The funny thing is, I appreciate those disappointments as well. They drive me on. Honestly, they make the achievements taste that much sweeter when they do come along.

There's one thing I've realised during my decade in the Premier League, though. I'm greedy for success. Goals, titles, Champions League trophies, the Club World Cup, League Cups, the FA Cup (one would be nice); any trophy we play for I want, because winning them, like my first Premier League in 2007, is the best feeling ever, but missing out, like in 2012, is the worst. I want to be brave enough, honest enough, hard-working enough to win more and more.

When I retire, I want to be thought of as a winner.

And I'm determined to get there.

In another decade's time, I want the fans to think of me as someone who gave it all.

I'll do whatever it takes for that to happen.

Like I said to some of the lads before I made my United debut in the Premier League:

EPILOGUE

Just give me the ball, I'll do it.
I'm not frightened …
I want it.

PICTURE CREDITS